author's success on the representation of "John Bull." The hearts and minds of his auditors were captivated, and proved, to demonstration, his skilful insight into human kind.

Were other witnesses necessary to confirm this truth, the whole dramatis personæ might be summoned as evidence, in whose characters human nature is powerfully described; and if, at times, too boldly for a reader's sober fancy, most judiciously adapted to that spirit which guides an audience.

It would be tedious to enumerate the beauties of this play, for it abounds with them. Its faults, in a moment, are numbered.

The prudence and good sense of Job Thornberry are so palpably deficient, in his having given to a little run-away, story-telling boy (as it is proved, and he might have suspected) ten guineas, the first earnings of his industry—that no one can wonder he becomes a bankrupt, or pity him when he does. In the common course of occurrences, ten guineas would redeem many a father of a family from bitter misery, and plunge many a youth into utter ruin. Yet nothing pleases an audience so much as a gift, let who will be the receiver. They should be broken of this vague propensity to give; and be taught, that charity without discrimination is a sensual enjoyment, and, like all sensuality, ought to be restrained: but that charity with discretion, is foremost amongst the virtues, and must not be contaminated with heedless profusion.—Still the author has shown such ingenuity in the event which arises from this incident, that those persons, who despise the silly generosity of Thornberry, are yet highly affected by the gratitude of Peregrine.

This comedy would read much better, but not act half so well, if it were all written in good English. It seems unreasonable to forbid an author to take advantage of any actor's peculiar abilities that may suit his convenience; and both Johnstone and Emery displayed abilities of the very first rate in the two characters they represented in "John Bull."—But to the author of "John Bull," whose genius may be animated to still higher exertions in the pursuit of fame, it may be said—Leave the distortion of language to men who cannot embellish it like yourself—and to women.

DRAMATIS PERSONÆ

Peregrine	Mr. Cooke.
Sir Simon Rochdale]	Mr. Blanchard.
Frank Rochdale	Mr. H. Johnston.
Williams	Mr. Klanert.
Lord Fitz-Balaam	Mr. Waddy.
Hon. Tom Shuffleton	Mr. Lewis
Job Thornberry	Mr. Fawcett.
John Bur	Mr. Atkins.
Dennis Brulgruddery	Mr. Johnstone.
Dan	Mr. Emery.
Mr. Pennyman	Mr. Davenport.
John	Mr. Abbot.
Robert	Mr. Truman.
Simon	Mr. Beverly.
Lady Caroline Braymore	Mrs. H. Johnston.

Mrs. Brulgruddery   Mrs. Davenport.
Mary Thornberry   Mrs. Gibbs.

SCENE:—Cornwall.

JOHN BULL

ACT THE FIRST

SCENE I

A Public House on a Heath

Over the Door the Sign of the Red Cow;—and the Name of "Dennis Brulgruddery."

Enter **DENNIS BRULGRUDDERY** and **DAN**, from the House. **DAN** opening the outward Shutters of the House.

DENNIS
A pretty blustratious night we have had! and the sun peeps through the fog this morning, like the copper pot in my kitchen.—Devil a traveller do I see coming to the Red Cow.

DAN
Na, measter!—nowt do pass by here, I do think, but the carrion crows.

DENNIS
Dan;—think you, will I be ruin'd?

DAN
Ees; past all condemption. We be the undonestest family in all Cornwall. Your ale be as dead as my grandmother; mistress do set by the fire, and sputter like an apple a-roasting; the pigs ha' gotten the measles; I be grown thinner nor an old sixpence; and thee hast drank up all the spirity liquors.

DENNIS
By my soul, I believe my setting up the Red Cow, a week ago, was a bit of a Bull!—but that's no odds. Haven't I been married these three months?—and who did I marry?

DAN
Why, a waddling woman, wi' a mulberry feace.

DENNIS
Have done with your blarney, Mr.

DAN
Think of the high blood in her veins, you bog trotter.

John Bull by George Colman the Younger

or, THE ENGLISHMAN'S FIRESIDE

A COMEDY, IN FIVE ACTS. AS PERFORMED AT THE THEATRE ROYAL, COVENT GARDEN.

George Colman the Younger was born on 21st October 1762, the son of George Colman the Elder, a noted and successful playwright and translator of Terence and Plautus among others.

Colman was educated at Westminster School before going on to University at Christ Church, Oxford, and then King's College, University of Aberdeen, before finally proceeding to Lincoln's Inn, London to become a student in Law.

In 1782 his first play 'The Female Dramatist' was premiered at his father's Haymarket theatre.

It appears that as early as 1784, Colman had entered into a runaway marriage with an actress, Clara Morris, to whose brother David Morris, he eventually sold his inherited share in the Haymarket theatre.

After her death he wrote many of the leading parts in his plays for Mrs Gibbs (née Logan), whom he was said to have secretly married after the death of his first wife.

His father, George Colman the Elder, was by now in failing health and was obliged to relinquish to his son the management of the Haymarket theatre in 1789, at a yearly salary of £600. Although Colman sought to emulate and build on the success of his father he was not quite of the same caliber.

On the death of his father in 1794, the Haymarket patent was continued to the son; but difficulties arose in his path, he was involved in litigation with Thomas Harris, and was unable to pay the running expenses of the performances at the Haymarket. In dire circumstances Colman was forced to seek sanctuary within the Rules of the King's Bench Prison. Although he would continue to manage the affairs of the theatre he would reside here for several years.

Released at last through the kindness of George IV, who had appointed him exon. of the Yeomen of the Guard, a dignity that Colman soon liquidated to the highest bidder.

In 1824 he was made examiner of plays by the Duke of Montrose, then the Lord Chamberlain. This granting of office caused widespread controversy amongst his peers who were appalled at his severe censorship and illiberal views, especially as his own works were often condemned as indecent. Apparently at times even the words 'heaven' and 'angel' were deemed to be offensive by him.

George Colman the Younger held this office until his death in Brompton, London on 17th October 1836 at the age of 73. He was buried alongside his father in Kensington Church.

Index of Contents

SCENE:—Cornwall.

JOHN BULL

ACT THE FIRST

SCENE I. A Public House on a Heath

ACT THE SECOND

SCENE I. A Library in the House of Sir Simon Rochdale; Books scattered on a Writing Table

SCENE III. An Apartment in Job Thornberry's House

ACT THE THIRD

SCENE I. Sir Simon Rochdale's Library

SCENE II. A mean Parlour at the Red Cow

ACT THE FOURTH

SCENE I. The Outside of the Red Cow

SCENE II

SCENE III. Another Apartment in Sir Simon Rochdale's House

ACT THE FIFTH

SCENE I. A Hall in the Manor-house

SCENE II. The Library

GEORGE COLMAN THE YOUNGER – A CONCISE BIBLIOGRAPHY

REMARKS by Mrs Inchbald

"Yet be not blindly guided by the throng;"The multitude is always in the wrong."

Roscommon surely meets with a bold contradiction in this comedy—for it was not only admired by the multitude, but the discerning few approved of that admiration.

The irresistible broad humour, which is the predominant quality of this drama, is so exquisitely interspersed with touches of nature more refined, with occasional flashes of wit, and with events so interesting, that, if the production is not of that perfect kind which the most rigid critic demands, he must still acknowledge it as a bond, given under the author's own hand, that he can, if he pleases, produce, in all its various branches, a complete comedy.

The introduction of farces into the entertainments of the theatre has been one cause of destroying that legitimate comedy, which such critics require. The eye, which has been accustomed to delight in paintings of caricature, regards a picture from real life as an insipid work. The extravagance of farce has given to the Town a taste for the pleasant convulsion of hearty laughter, and smiles are contemned, as the tokens of insipid amusement.

To know the temper of the times with accuracy, is one of the first talents requisite to a dramatic author. The works of other authors may be reconsidered a week, a month, or a year after a first perusal, and regain their credit by an increase of judgment bestowed upon their reader; but the dramatist, once brought before the public, must please at first sight, or never be seen more. There is no reconsideration in his case—no judgment to expect beyond the decree of the moment: and he must direct his force against the weakness, as well as the strength, of his jury. He must address their habits, passions, and prejudices, as the only means to gain this sudden conquest of their minds and hearts. Such was the

DAN
Ees; I always do, when I do look at her nose.

DENNIS
Never you mind Mrs. Brulgruddery's nose. Was'nt she fat widow to Mr. Skinnygauge, the lean exciseman of Lestweithel? and did'nt her uncle, who is fifteenth cousin to a Cornish Baronet, say he'd leave her no money, if he ever happen'd to have any, because she had disgraced her parentage, by marrying herself to a taxman? Bathershan, man, and don't you think he'll help us out of the mud, now her second husband is an Irish jontleman, bred and born?

DAN
He, he! Thee be'st a rum gentleman.

DENNIS
Troth, and myself, Mr. Dennis Brulgruddery, was brought up to the church.

DAN
Why, zure!

DENNIS
You may say that, I open'd the pew doors, in Belfast.

DAN
And what made 'em to turn thee out o'the treade?

DENNIS
I snored in sermon time. Dr. Snufflebags, the preacher, said I woke the rest of the congregation. Arrah, Dan, don't I see a tall customer stretching out his arms in the fog?

DAN
Na; that be the road-post.

DENNIS
'Faith, and so it is. Och! when I was turn'd out of my snug birth at Belfast, the tears ran down my eighteen year old cheeks, like buttermilk.

DAN
Pshaw, man! nonsense! Thee'dst never get another livelihood by crying.

DENNIS
Yes, I did; I cried oysters. Then I pluck'd up—what's that? a customer!

DAN [Looking out]
Na, a donkey.

DENNIS
Well, then I pluck'd up a parcel of my courage, and I carried arms.

DAN

Waunds! what, a musket?

DENNIS

No; a reaping hook. I cut my way half through England: till a German learn'd me physic, at a fair in Devonshire.

DAN

What, poticary's stuff?

DENNIS

I studied it in Doctor Von Quolchigronck's booth, at Plympton. He cured the yellow glanders, and restored prolification to families who wanted an heir. I was of mighty use to him as an assistant.

DAN

Were you indeed!

DENNIS

But, somehow, the doctor and I had a quarrel; so I gave him something, and parted.

DAN

And what didst thee give him, pray?

DENNIS

I gave him a black-eye; and set up for myself at Lestweithel; where Mr. Skinnygauge, the exciseman, was in his honeymoon.—Poor soul! he was my patient, and died one day: but his widow had such a neat notion of my subscriptions, that in three weeks, she was Mrs. Brulgruddery.

DAN

He, he! so you jumped into the old man's money?

DENNIS

Only a dirty hundred pounds. Then her brother-in-law, bad luck to him! kept the Red Cow, upon Muckslush Heath, till his teeth chatter'd him out of the world, in an ague.

DAN

Why, that be this very house.

DENNIS

Ould Nick fly away with the roof of it! I took the remainder of the lease, per advice of my bride, Mrs. Brulgruddery: laid out her goodlooking hundred pound for the furniture, and the goodwill; bought three pigs, that are going into a consumption; took a sarvingman—

DAN

That's I.—I be a going into a consumption too, sin you hired me.

DENNIS

And devil a soul has darken'd my doors for a pot of beer since I have been a publican.

DAN
See!—See, mun, see! yon's a traveller, sure as eggs!—and a coming this road.

DENNIS
Och, hubbaboo! a customer, at last! St. Patrick send he may be a pure dry one! Be alive, Dan, be alive! run and tell him there's elegant refreshment at the Red Cow.

DAN
I will—Oh, dang it, I doesn't mind a bit of a lie.

DENNIS
And harkye:—say there's an accomplish'd landlord.

DAN
Ees—and a genteel waiter; but he'll see that.

DENNIS
And, Dan;—sink that little bit of a thunder storm, that has sour'd all the beer, you know.

DAN
What, dost take me for an oaf? Dang me, if he han't been used to drink vinegar, he'll find it out fast enow of himsel, Ise warrant un!

[Exit.

DENNIS
Wife!—I must tell her the joyful news—Mrs. Brulgruddery! my dear!—Devil choak my dear!—she's as deaf as a trunk-maker—Mrs. Brulgruddery!

[Enter **MRS BRULGRUDDERY**

MRS BRULGRUDDERY
And what do you want, now, with Mrs. Brulgruddery? What's to become of us? tell me that. How are we going on, I shou'd like to know?

DENNIS
Mighty like a mile-stone—standing still, at this present writing.

MRS BRULGRUDDERY
A pretty situation we are in truly!

DENNIS
Yes;—upon Muckslush Heath, and be damn'd to it.

MRS BRULGRUDDERY
And, where is the fortune I brought you?

DENNIS
All swallow'd up by the Red Cow.

MRS BRULGRUDDERY
Ah! had you follow'd my advice, we shou'd never have been in such a quandary.

DENNIS
Tunder and turf! didn't yourself advise me to take this public house?

MRS BRULGRUDDERY
No matter for that. I had a relation who always kept it. But, who advised you to drink out all the brandy?

DENNIS
No matter for that. I had a relation who always drank it.

MRS BRULGRUDDERY [Crying]
Ah! my poor dear Mr. Skinnygauge never brought tears into my eyes, as you do!

DENNIS
I know that—I saw you at his funeral.

MRS BRULGRUDDERY
You're a monster!

DENNIS
Am I?—Keep it to yourself, then, my lambkin.

MRS BRULGRUDDERY
You'll be the death of me; you know you will.

DENNIS
Look up, my sweet Mrs. Brulgruddery! while I give you a small morsel of consolation.

MRS BRULGRUDDERY
Consolation indeed!

DENNIS
Yes—There's a customer coming.

MRS BRULGRUDDERY [Brightening]
What!

DENNIS
A customer. Turn your neat jolly face over the Heath, yonder. Look at Dan, towing him along, as snug as a cock salmon into a fish basket.

MRS BRULGRUDDERY

Jimminy, and so there is! Oh, my dear Dennis! But I knew how it would be, if you had but a little patience. Remember, it was all by my advice you took the Red Cow.

DENNIS
Och ho! it was, was it?

MRS BRULGRUDDERY
I'll run, and spruce myself up a bit. Aye, aye, I hav'n't prophesied a customer to-day for nothing.

[Goes into the House.

DENNIS
Troth, and it's prophesying on the sure side, to foretell a thing when it has happen'd.

[Enter **DAN**, conducting **PEREGRINE**—**PEREGRINE** carrying a small Trunk under his Arm.

PEREGRINE
I am indifferent about accommodations.

DAN
Our'n be a comfortable parlour, zur: you'll find it clean: for I wash'd un down mysen, wringing wet, five minutes ago.

PEREGRINE
You have told me so, twenty times.

DAN
This be the Red Cow, zur, as you may see by the pictur; and here be measter—he'll treat ye in a hospital manner, zur, and show you a deal o' contention.

DENNIS
I'll be bound, sir, you'll get good entertainment, whether you are a man or a horse.

PEREGRINE
You may lodge me as either, friend. I can sleep as well in a stable as a bedchamber; for travel has season'd me.—Since I have preserved this—

[Half aside, and pointing to the Trunk under his Arm.

I can lay my head upon it with tranquility, and repose any where.

DENNIS
'Faith, it seems a mighty decent, hard bolster. What is it stuff'd with, I wonder?

PEREGRINE
That which keeps the miser awake—money.

DAN

Wauns! all that money!

DENNIS
I'd be proud, sir, to know your upholsterer—he should make me a feather bed gratis of the same pretty materials. If that was all my own, I'd sleep like a pig, though I'm married to Mrs. Brulgruddery.

PEREGRINE
I shall sleep better, because it is not my own.

DENNIS
Your own's in a snugger place, then? safe from the sharks of this dirty world, and be hang'd to 'em!

PEREGRINE
Except the purse in my pocket, 'tis, now, I fancy, in a place most frequented by the sharks of this world.

DENNIS
London, I suppose?

PEREGRINE
The bottom of the sea.

DENNIS
By my soul, that's a watering place—and you'll find sharks there, sure enough in all conscience.
Enter Mrs. Brulgruddery.

MRS BRULGRUDDERY
What would you chuse to take, sir, after your walk this raw morning? We have any thing you desire.

DENNIS [Aside]
Yes, we have any thing. Any thing's nothing, they say.

MRS BRULGRUDDERY
Dan, bustle about; and see the room ready, and all tidy; do you hear?

DAN
I wull.

MRS BRULGRUDDERY
What would you like to drink, sir?

PEREGRINE
O, mine is an accommodating palate, hostess. I have swallowed burgundy with the French, hollands with the Dutch, sherbet with a Turk, sloe juice with an Englishman, and water with a simple Gentoo.

DAN [Going]
Dang me, but he's a rum customer! It's my opinion, he'll take a fancy to our sour beer.

[Exit into the House

PEREGRINE
Is your house far from the sea-shore?

MRS BRULGRUDDERY
About three miles, sir.

PEREGRINE
So!—And I have wandered upon the heath four hours, before day-break.

MRS BRULGRUDDERY
Lackaday! has any thing happened to you, sir?

PEREGRINE
Shipwreck—that's all.

MRS BRULGRUDDERY
Mercy on us! cast away?

PEREGRINE
On your coast, here.

DENNIS
Then, compliment apart, sir, you take a ducking as if you had been used to it.

PEREGRINE
Life's a lottery, friend; and man should make up his mind to the blanks. On what part of Cornwall am I thrown?

MRS BRULGRUDDERY
We are two miles from Penzance, sir.

PEREGRINE
Ha!—from Penzance!—that's lucky!

MRS BRULGRUDDERY [Aside to **DENNIS**]
Lucky!—Then he'll go on, without drinking at our house.

DENNIS
A hem!—Sir, there has been a great big thunder storm at Penzance, and all the beer in the town's as thick as mustard.

PEREGRINE
I feel chill'd—get me a glass of brandy.

DENNIS [Aloud to his **WIFE**]
Och, the devil!
Bring the brandy bottle for the jontleman, my jewel.

MRS BRULGRUDDERY [Apart]
Dont you know you've emptied it, you sot, you!

DENNIS [Apart]
Draw a mug of beer—I'll palaver him.

MRS BRULGRUDDERY [Apart, and going]
Ah! if you would but follow my advice!

[Exit into the House.

DENNIS
You see that woman that's gone sir,—she's my wife, poor soul! She has but one misfortune, and that's a wapper.

PEREGRINE
What's that?

DENNIS
We had as a neat a big bottle of brandy, a week ago—and damn the drop's left. But I say nothing—she's my wife, poor creature! and she can tell who drank it. Would'nt you like a sup of sour—I mean, of our strong beer?

PEREGRINE
Pshaw! no matter what. Tell me, is a person of the name of Thornberry still living in Penzance?

DENNIS
Is it one Mr. Thornberry you are asking after?

PEREGRINE
Yes. When I first saw him (indeed, it was the first time and the last), he had just begun to adventure humbly in trade. His stock was very slender, but his neighbours accounted him a kindly man—and I know they spoke the truth. Thirty years ago, after half an hour's intercourse, which proved to me his benevolent nature, I squeezed his hand, and parted.

DENNIS
Thirty years! 'Faith, after half an hour's dish of talk, that's a reasonable long time to remember!

PEREGRINE
Not at all; for he did me a genuine service; and gratitude writes the records in the heart, that, till it ceases to beat, they may live in the memory.

[Enter **MRS BRULGRUDDERY**, with a Mug of Beer.

MRS BRULGRUDDERY [Apart to **DENNIS**]
What have you said about the brandy bottle?

DENNIS [Apart]
I told him you broke it, one day.

MRS BRULGRUDDERY [Apart]
Ah! I am always the shelter for your sins.

DENNIS
Hush!—
[To **PEREGRINE**]
You know, sir, I—hem!—I mention'd to you poor Mrs. Brulgruddery's misfortune.

PEREGRINE
Ha, ha! you did indeed, friend.

MRS BRULGRUDDERY
I am very sorry, sir, but—

DENNIS
Be asy, my lambkin! the jontleman excuses it. You are not the first that has crack'd a bottle, you know.—
Here's your beer, sir.
[Taking it from his **WIFE**]
I'm not of a blushing nation, or I'd be shame-faced to give it him.—
[Aside]
My jewel, the jontleman was asking after one Mr. Thornberry.

[Delaying to give the Beer.

MRS BRULGRUDDERY
What! old Job Thornberry of Penzance, sir?

PEREGRINE
The very same. You know him, then?

MRS BRULGRUDDERY [To **DENNIS**]
Very well, by hearsay, sir. He has lived there upwards of thirty years. A very thriving man now, and well to do in the world;—as others might be, too, if they would but follow my advice.

PEREGRINE
I rejoice to hear it. Give me the beer, Landlord; I'll drink his health in humble malt, then hasten to visit him.

DENNIS [Aside]
By St. Patrick, then, you'll make wry faces on the road.

[Gives him the mug.

[As **PEREGRINE** is about to drink, a Shriek is heard at a small Distance.

PEREGRINE
Ha! the voice of a female in distress? Then 'tis a man's business to fly to her protection.

[Dashes the Mug on the Ground. Exit.

MRS BRULGRUDDERY
Wheugh! what a whirligigg! Why, Dennis, the man's mad!

DENNIS
I think that thing.

MRS BRULGRUDDERY
He has thrown down all the beer, before he tasted a drop.

DENNIS
That's it: if he had chuck'd it away afterwards, I shou'dn't have wonder'd.

MRS BRULGRUDDERY
Here he comes again;—and, I declare, with a young woman leaning on his shoulder.

DENNIS
A young woman! let me have a bit of a peep.

[Looking out.

Och, the crater! Och, the—

MRS BRULGRUDDERY
Heyday! I should'n't have thought of your peeping after a young woman, indeed!

DENNIS
Be asy, Mrs. Brulgruddery! it's a way we have in Ireland.—There's a face!

MRS BRULGRUDDERY
Well, and hav'n't I a face, pray?

DENNIS
That you have, my lambkin! You have had one these fifty years, I'll bound for you.

MRS BRULGRUDDERY
Fifty years! you are the greatest brute that ever dug potatoes.

[Re-enter **PEREGRINE**, supporting **MARY**.

PEREGRINE
This way. Cheer your spirits; the ruffian with whom I saw you struggling, has fled across the Heath; but his speed prevented my saving your property. Was your money, too, in the parcel with your clothes?

MARY
All I possessed in the world, sir;—and he has so frighten'd me!—Indeed. I thank you, sir; indeed I do!

PEREGRINE
Come, come, compose yourself. Whither are you going, pretty one?

MARY
I must not tell, sir.

PEREGRINE
Then whither do you come from?

MARY
No body must know, sir.

PEREGRINE
Umph! Then your proceedings, child, are a secret?

MARY
Yes, sir.

PEREGRINE
Yet you appear to need a friend to direct them. A heath is a rare place to find one: in the absence of a better, confide in me.

MARY
You forget that you are a stranger, sir.

PEREGRINE
I always do—when the defenceless want my assistance.

MARY
But, perhaps you might betray me, sir.

PEREGRINE
Never—by the honour of a man!

MARY
Pray don't swear by that, sir! for, then, you'll betray me, I'm certain.

PEREGRINE
Have you ever suffered from treachery, then, poor innocence?

MARY
Yes, sir.

PEREGRINE
And may not one of your own sex have been treacherous to you?

MARY
No, sir; I'm very sure he was a man.

DENNIS
Oh, the blackguard!

MRS BRULGRUDDERY
Hold your tongue, do!

PEREGRINE
Listen to me, child. I would proffer you friendship, for your own sake—for the sake of benevolence. When ages, indeed, are nearly equal, nature is prone to breathe so warmly on the blossoms of a friendship between the sexes, that the fruit is desire; but time, fair one, is scattering snow on my temples, while Hebe waves her freshest ringlets over yours. Rely, then, on one who has numbered years sufficient to correct his passions; who has encountered difficulties enough to teach him sympathy; and who would stretch forth his hand to a wandering female, and shelter her like a father.

MARY [Weeping]
Oh, sir! I do want protection sadly indeed! I am very miserable!

PEREGRINE
Come, do not droop. The cause of your distress, perhaps, is trifling; but, light gales of adversity will make women weep. A woman's tear falls like the dew that zephyrs shake from roses.—Nay, confide in me.

MARY [Looking round]
I will, sir; but—

PEREGRINE
Leave us a little, honest friends.

DENNIS
A hem!—Come, Mrs. Brulgruddery! let you and I pair off, my lambkin!

MRS BRULGRUDDERY [Going]
Ah! she's no better than she should be, I'll warrant her.

DENNIS
By the powers, she's well enough though, for all that.

[Exeunt **DENNIS** and **MRS BRULGRUDDERY** into the House.

PEREGRINE
Now, sweet one, your name?

MARY
Mary, sir.

PEREGRINE
What else?

MARY
Don't ask me that, sir: my poor father might be sorry it was mentioned, now.

PEREGRINE
Have you quitted your father, then?

MARY
I left his house at day-break, this morning, sir.

PEREGRINE
What is he?

MARY
A tradesman in the neighbouring town, sir.

PEREGRINE
Is he aware of your departure?

MARY
No, sir,

PEREGRINE
And your mother—?

MARY
I was very little, when she died, sir.

PEREGRINE
Has your father, since her death, treated you with cruelty?

MARY
He? Oh, bless him! no! he is the kindest father that ever breathed, sir.

PEREGRINE
How must such a father be agonized by the loss of his child!

MARY
Pray, sir, don't talk of that!

PEREGRINE
Why did you fly from him?

MARY
Sir, I—I—but that's my story, sir.

PEREGRINE

Relate it, then.

MARY

Yes, sir.—You must know, then, sir, that—there was a young gentleman in this neighbourhood, that—O dear, sir, I'm quite ashamed!

PEREGRINE

Come, child, I will relieve you from the embarrassment of narration, and sum up your history in one word;—love.

MARY

That's the beginning of it, sir; but a great deal happen'd afterwards.

PEREGRINE

And who is the hero of your story, my poor girl?

MARY

The hero of—? O, I understand—he is much above me in fortune, sir. To be sure, I should have thought of that, before he got such power over my heart, to make me so wretched, now he has deserted me.

PEREGRINE

He would have thought of that, had his own heart been generous.

MARY

He is reckon'd very generous, sir; he can afford to be so. When the old gentleman dies, he will have all the great family estate. I am going to the house, now, sir.

PEREGRINE

For what purpose?

MARY

To try if I can see him for the last time, sir: to tell him I shall always pray for his happiness, when I am far away from a place which he has made it misery for me to abide in;—and to beg him to give me a little supply of money, now I am pennyless, and from home, to help me to London; where I may get into service, and nobody will know me.

PEREGRINE

And what are his reasons, child, for thus deserting you?

MARY

He sent me his reasons, by letter, yesterday, sir. He is to be married next week, to a lady of high fortune. His father, he says, insists upon it. I know I am born below him; but after the oaths we plighted, Heaven knows, the news was a sad, sad shock to me! I did not close my eyes last night; my poor brain was burning; and, as soon as day broke, I left the house of my dear father, whom I should tremble to look at, when he discover'd my story;—which I could not long conceal from him.

PEREGRINE

Poor, lovely, heart-bruised wanderer! O wealthy despoilers of humble innocence! splendid murderers of virtue; who make your vice your boast, and fancy female ruin a feather in your caps of vanity—single out a victim you have abandoned, and, in your hours of death, contemplate her!—view her, care-worn, friendless, pennyless;—hear her tale of sorrows, fraught with her remorse,—her want,—a hard world's scoffs, her parents' anguish;—then, if ye dare, look inward upon your own bosoms; and if they be not conscience proof what must be your compunctions!—Who is his father, child?

MARY
Sir Simon Rochdale, sir, of the Manor-house, hard by.

PEREGRINE [Surprised]
Indeed!

MARY
Perhaps you know him, sir?

PEREGRINE
I have heard of him;—and, on your account, shall visit him.

MARY
Oh, pray, sir, take care what you do! if you should bring his son into trouble, by mentioning me, I should never, never forgive myself.

PEREGRINE
Trust to my caution.—Promise only to remain at this house, till I return from a business which calls me, immediately, two miles hence; I will hurry back to pursue measures for your welfare, with more hope of success, than your own weak means, poor simplicity, are likely to effect. What say you?

MARY
I hardly know what to say, sir—you seem good,—and I am little able to help myself.

PEREGRINE
You consent, then?

MARY
Yes, sir.

PEREGRINE [Calling]
Landlord!

[Enter **DENNIS**, from the Door of the House—**MRS BRULGRUDDERY** following.

DENNIS
Did you call, sir?—Arrah, now, Mrs. Brulgruddery, you are peeping after the young woman yourself.

MRS BRULGRUDDERY
I chuse it.

PEREGRINE
Prepare your room, good folks; and get the best accommodation you can for this young person.

DENNIS
That I will, with all my heart and soul, sir.

MRS BRULGRUDDERY [Sulkily]
I don't know that we have any room at all, for my part.

DENNIS
Whew! She's in her tantrums.

MRS BRULGRUDDERY
People of repute can't let in young women (found upon a heath, forsooth), without knowing who's who. I have learn'd the ways of the world, sir.

PEREGRINE
So it seems:—which too often teach you to over-rate the little good you can do in it: and to shut the door when the distressed entreat you to throw it open. But I have learnt the ways of the world too.

[Taking out his Purse.

I shall return in a few hours. Provide all the comforts you can; and here are a couple of guineas, to send for any refreshments you have not in the house.

[Giving Money.

DENNIS
Mighty pretty handsel for the Red Cow, my lambkin!

MRS BRULGRUDDERY
A couple of guineas! Lord, sir! if I thought you had been such a gentleman!—Pray, miss, walk in! your poor dear, little feet must be quite wet with our nasty roads. I beg pardon, sir; but character's every thing in our business; and I never lose sight of my own credit.

DENNIS
That you don't—till you see other people's ready money.

PEREGRINE
Go in, child. I shall soon be with you again.

MARY
You will return, then, sir?

PEREGRINE
Speedily. Rely on me.

MARY

I shall, sir;—I am sure I may. Heaven bless you, sir!

MRS BRULGRUDDERY [Courtesying]
This way, miss; this way!

[Exeunt **MARY** and **LANDLADY**, into the House.

DENNIS
Long life to your honour, for protecting the petticoats! sweet creatures! I'd like to protect them myself, by bushels.

PEREGRINE
Can you get me a guide, friend, to conduct me to Penzance?

DENNIS
Get you a guide! There's Dan, my servant, shall skip before you over the bogs, like a grasshopper. Oh, by the powers! my heart's full to see your generosity, and I owe you a favour in return:—never you call for any of my beer, till I get a fresh tap.

[Exit into the House.

PEREGRINE
Now for my friend, Thornberry; then hither again, to interest myself in the cause of this unfortunate: for which many would call me Quixote; many would cant out "shame!" but I care not for the stoics, nor the puritans. Genuine nature and unsophisticated morality, that turn disgusted from the rooted adepts in vice, have ever a reclaiming tear to shed on the children of error. Then, let the sterner virtues, that allow no plea for human frailty, stalk on to paradise without me! The mild associate of my journey thither shall be charity:—and my pilgrimage to the shrine of mercy will not, I trust, be worse performed for having aided the weak, on my way, who have stumbled in their progress.

[Enter **DAN**, from the House.

DAN
I be ready, zur.

PEREGRINE
For what, friend?

DAN
Measter says you be a-going to Penzance; if you be agreeable, I'll keep you company.

PEREGRINE
Oh—the guide. You belong to the house?

DAN
Ees, zur; Ise enow to do: I be head waiter and hostler:—only we never have no horses, nor customers.

PEREGRINE

The path I fancy, is difficult to find. Do you never deviate?

DAN
Na, zur,—I always whistles.

PEREGRINE
Come on, friend.—It seems a dreary rout: but how cheerily the eye glances over a sterile tract, when the habitation of a benefactor, whom we are approaching to requite, lies in the perspective!

[Exeunt.

SCENE I

A Library in the House of Sir Simon Rochdale; Books scattered on a Writing Table

Enter **TOM SHUFFLETON**.

TOM SHUFFLETON
No body up yet? I thought so.

[Enter **SERVANT**.

Ah, John, is it you? How d'ye do, John?

JOHN
Thank your honour, I—

TOM SHUFFLETON
Yes, you look so. Sir Simon Rochdale in bed? Mr. Rochdale not risen? Well! no matter; I have travelled all night, though, to be with them. How are they?

JOHN
Sir, they are both—

TOM SHUFFLETON
I'm glad to hear it. Pay the postboy for me.

JOHN
Yes, sir. I beg pardon, sir; but when your honour last left us—

TOM SHUFFLETON
Owed you three pound five. I remember: have you down in my memorandums—Honourable Tom Shuffleton debtor to— What's your name?

JOHN
My christian name, sir, is—

TOM SHUFFLETON
Muggins—I recollect. Pay the postboy, Muggins. And, harkye, take particular care of the chaise: I borrowed it of my friend, Bobby Fungus, who sprang up a peer, in the last bundle of Barons: if a single knob is knocked out of his new coronets, he'll make me a sharper speech than ever he'll produce in parliament. And, John!

JOHN
Sir!

TOM SHUFFLETON
What was I going to say?

JOHN
Indeed, sir, I can't tell.

TOM SHUFFLETON
No more can I. 'Tis the fashion to be absent—that's the way I forgot your little bill. There, run along.

[Exit **JOHN**.

I've the whirl of Bobby's chaise in my head still. Cursed fatiguing, posting all night, through Cornish roads, to obey the summons of friendship! Convenient, in some respects, for all that. If all loungers, of slender revenues, like mine, could command a constant succession of invitations, from men of estates in the country, how amazingly it would tend to the thinning of Bond Street!

[Throws himself into a Chair near the Writing Table.

Let me see—what has Sir Simon been reading?—"Burn's Justice"—true; the old man's reckoned the ablest magistrate in the county. he hasn't cut open the leaves, I see. "Chesterfield's Letters"—pooh! his system of education is extinct: Belcher and the Butcher have superseded it. "Clarendon's History of—."

[Enter **SIR SIMON ROCHDALE**.

SIR SIMON
Ah, my dear Tom Shuffleton!

TOM SHUFFLETON
Baronet! how are you?

SIR SIMON
Such expedition is kind now! You got my letter at Bath, and—

TOM SHUFFLETON
Saw it was pressing:—here I am. Cut all my engagements for you, and came off like a shot.

SIR SIMON

Thank you: thank you, heartily!

TOM SHUFFLETON

Left every thing at sixes and sevens.

SIR SIMON

Gad, I'm sorry if—

TOM SHUFFLETON

Don't apologize;—nobody does, now. Left all my bills, in the place, unpaid.

SIR SIMON

Bless me! I've made it monstrous inconvenient!

TOM SHUFFLETON

Not a bit—I give you my honour, I did'nt find it inconvenient at all. How is Frank Rochdale?

SIR SIMON

Why, my son is'nt up yet; and before he's stirring, do let me talk to you, my dear Tom Shuffleton! I have something near my heart, that—

TOM SHUFFLETON

Don't talk about your heart, Baronet;—feeling's quite out of fashion.

SIR SIMON

Well, then, I'm interested in—

TOM SHUFFLETON

Aye, stick to that. We make a joke of the heart, now-a-days; but when a man mentions his interest, we know he's in earnest.

SIR SIMON

Zounds! I am in earnest. Let me speak, and call my motives what you will.

TOM SHUFFLETON

Speak—but don't be in a passion. We are always cool at the clubs: the constant habit of ruining one another, teaches us temper. Explain.

SIR SIMON

Well, I will. You know, my dear Tom, how much I admire your proficiency in the New school of breeding;—you are, what I call, one of the highest finished fellows of the present day.

TOM SHUFFLETON

Psha! Baronet; you flatter.

SIR SIMON

No, I don't; only in extolling the merits of the newest fashion'd manners and morals, I am sometimes puzzled, by the plain gentlemen, who listen to me, here in the country, most consumedly.

TOM SHUFFLETON
I don't doubt it.

SIR SIMON
Why, 'twas but t'other morning, I was haranguing old Sir Noah Starchington, in my library, and explaining to him the shining qualities of a dasher, of the year eighteen hundred and three; and what do you think he did?

TOM SHUFFLETON
Fell asleep.

SIR SIMON
No; he pull'd down an English dictionary; when (if you'll believe me! he found my definition of stylish living, under the word "insolvency;" a fighting crop turn'd out a "dock'd bull dog;" and modern gallantry, "adultery and seduction."

TOM SHUFFLETON
Noah Starchington is a damn'd old twaddler.—But the fact is, Baronet, we improve. We have voted many qualities to be virtues, now, that they never thought of calling virtues formerly. The rising generation wants a new dictionary, damnably.

SIR SIMON
Deplorably, indeed! You can't think, my dear Tom, what a scurvy figure you, and the dashing fellows of your kidney, make in the old ones. But you have great influence over my son Frank; and want you to exert it. You are his intimate—you come here, and pass two or three months at a time, you know.

TOM SHUFFLETON
Yes—this is a pleasant house.

SIR SIMON
You ride his horses, as if they were your own.

TOM SHUFFLETON
Yes—he keeps a good stable.

SIR SIMON
You drink our claret with him, till his head aches.

TOM SHUFFLETON
Your's is famous claret, Baronet.

SIR SIMON
You worm out his secrets: you win his money; you—. In short, you are—

TOM SHUFFLETON

His friend, according to the next new dictionary. That's what you mean, Sir Simon.

SIR SIMON
Exactly.—But, let me explain. Frank, if he doesn't play the fool, and spoil all, is going to be married.

TOM SHUFFLETON
To how much?

SIR SIMON
Damn it, now, how like a modern man of the world that is! Formerly they would have asked to who.

TOM SHUFFLETON
We never do, now;—fortune's every thing. We say, "a good match," at the west end of the town, as they say "a good man," in the city;—the phrase refers merely to money. Is she rich?

SIR SIMON
Four thousand a-year.

TOM SHUFFLETON
What a devilish desirable woman! Frank's a happy dog!

SIR SIMON
He's a miserable puppy. He has no more notion, my dear Tom, of a modern "good match," than Eve had of pin money.

TOM SHUFFLETON
What are his objections to it?

SIR SIMON
I have smoked him; but he doesn't know that;—a silly, sly amour, in another quarter.

TOM SHUFFLETON
An amour! That's a very unfashionable reason for declining matrimony.

SIR SIMON
You know his romantic flights. The blockhead, I believe, is so attach'd, I shou'dn't wonder if he flew off at a tangent, and married the girl that has bewitch'd him.

TOM SHUFFLETON
Who is she?

SIR SIMON
She—hem!—she lives with her father, in Penzance.

TOM SHUFFLETON
And who is he?

SIR SIMON

He—upon my soul I'm asham'd to tell you.

TOM SHUFFLETON
Don't be asham'd; we never blush at any thing, in the New School.

SIR SIMON
Damn me, my dear Tom, if he isn't a brazier!

TOM SHUFFLETON
The devil!

SIR SIMON
A dealer in kitchen candlesticks, coal skuttles, coppers, and cauldrons.

TOM SHUFFLETON
And is the girl pretty?

SIR SIMON
So they tell me;—a plump little devil, as round as a tea kettle.

TOM SHUFFLETON
I'll be after the brazier's daughter, to-morrow.

SIR SIMON
But you have weight with him. Talk to him, my dear Tom—reason with him; try your power, Tom, do!

TOM SHUFFLETON
I don't much like plotting with the father against the son—that's reversing the New School, Baronet.

SIR SIMON
But it will serve Frank: it will serve me, who wish to serve you. And to prove that I do wish it, I have been keeping something in embryo for you, my dear Tom Shuffleton, against your arrival.

TOM SHUFFLETON
For me?

SIR SIMON
When you were last leaving us, if you recollect, you mention'd, in a kind of a way, a—a sort of an intention of a loan, of an odd five hundred pounds.

TOM SHUFFLETON
Did I? I believe I might.—When I intend to raise money, I always give my friends the preference.

SIR SIMON
I told you I was out of cash then, I remember.

TOM SHUFFLETON
Yes: that's just what I told you, I remember.

SIR SIMON [Presenting it]
I have the sum floating by me, now, and much at your service.

TOM SHUFFLETON [Taking it]
Why, as it's lying idle, Baronet, I—I—don't much care if I employ it.

SIR SIMON
Use your interest with Frank, now.

TOM SHUFFLETON
Rely on me.—Shall I give you my note?

SIR SIMON
No, my dear Tom, that's an unnecessary trouble.

TOM SHUFFLETON
Why that's true—with one who knows me so well as you.

SIR SIMON
Your verbal promise to pay, is quite as good.

TOM SHUFFLETON [Going]
I'll see if Frank's stirring.

SIR SIMON [Going]
And I must talk to my steward.

TOM SHUFFLETON
Baronet!

SIR SIMON [Returning]
Eh?

TOM SHUFFLETON
Pray, do you employ the phrase, "verbal promise to pay," according to the reading of old dictionaries, or as it's the fashion to use it at present.

SIR SIMON
Oh, damn it, chuse your own reading, and I'm content.

[Exeunt severally.

SCENE II

A Dressing Room

FRANK ROCHDALE writing; **WILLIAMS** attending.

FRANK [Throwing down the Pen]
It don't signify—I cannot write. I blot, and tear; and tear, and blot; and—. Come here, Williams. Do let me hear you, once more. Why the devil don't you come here?

WILLIAMS
I am here, sir.

FRANK
Well, well; my good fellow, tell me. You found means to deliver her the letter yesterday?

WILLIAMS
Yes, sir.

FRANK
And, she read it—and—did you say, she—she was very much affected, when she read it?

WILLIAMS
I told you last night, sir;—she look'd quite death struck, as I may say.

FRANK [Much affected]
Did—did she weep, Williams?

WILLIAMS
No, sir; but I did afterwards—I don't know what ail'd me; but, when I got out of the house, into the street, I'll be hang'd if I did'nt cry like a child.

FRANK
You are an honest fellow, Williams.

[A Knock at the Door of the Room.

See who is at the door.

[**WILLIAMS** opens the Door.

[Enter **JOHN**.

WILLIAMS
Well, what's the matter?

JOHN
There's a man in the porter's lodge, says he won't go away without speaking to Mr. Francis.

FRANK
See who it is, Williams.

Send him to me, if necessary; but don't let me be teased, without occasion.

WILLIAMS
I'll take care, sir.

[Exeunt **WILLIAMS** and **JOHN**.

FRANK
Must I marry this woman, whom my father has chosen for me; whom I expect here to-morrow? And must I, then, be told 'tis criminal to love my poor, deserted Mary, because our hearts are illicitly attach'd? Illicit for the heart? fine phraseology! Nature disowns the restriction; I cannot smother her dictates with the polity of governments, and fall in, or out of love, as the law directs.

[Enter **DENNIS BRULGRUDDERY**.

Well, friend, who do you come from?

DENNIS
I come from the Red Cow, sir.

FRANK
The Red Cow?

DENNIS
Yes, sir!—upon Muckslush Heath—hard by your honour's father's house, here. I'd be proud of your custom, sir, and all the good looking family's.

FRANK [Impatiently]
Well, well, your business?

DENNIS
That's what the porter ax'd me, "Tell me your business, honest man," says he—"I'll see you damn'd first, sir," says I:—"I'll tell it your betters;—and that's Mr. Francis Rochdale, Esquire."

FRANK
Zounds! then, why don't you tell it? I am Mr. Francis Rochdale.—Who the devil sent you here?

DENNIS
Troth, sir, it was good nature whisper'd me to come to your honour: but I believe I've disremembered her directions, for damn the bit do you seem acquainted with her.

FRANK
Well, my good friend, I don't mean to be violent; only be so good as to explain your business.

DENNIS
Oh, with all the pleasure in life.—Give me good words, and I'm as aisy as an ould glove: but bite my nose off with mustard, and have at you with pepper,—that's my way.—There's a little crature at my house;—

she's crying her eyes out;—and she won't get such another pair at the Red Cow; for I've left nobody with her but Mrs. Brulgruddery.

FRANK
With her? with who? Who are you talking off?

DENNIS
I'd like to know her name myself, sir;—but I have heard but half of it;—and that's Mary.

FRANK
Mary!—Can it be she?—Wandering on a heath! seeking refuge in a wretched hovel!

DENNIS
A hovel! O fie for shame of yourself, to misbecall a genteel tavern! I'd have you to know my parlour is clean sanded once a week.

FRANK
Tell me, directly—what brought her to your house?

DENNIS
By my soul, it was Adam's own carriage: a ten-toed machine the haymakers keep in Ireland.

FRANK
Damn it, fellow, don't trifle, but tell your story; and, if you can, intelligibly.

DENNIS
Don't be bothering my brains, then, or you'll get it as clear as mud. Sure the young crature can't fly away from the Red Cow, while I'm explaining to you the rights on't—Didn't she promise the gentleman to stay till he came back?

FRANK
Promised a gentleman!—Who?—who is the gentleman?

DENNIS
Arrah, now, where did you larn manners? Would you ax a customer his birth, parentage, and education? "Heaven bless you, sir, you'll come back again?" says she—"That's what I will, before you can say, parsnips, my darling," says he.

FRANK
Damnation! what does this mean?—explain your errand, clearly, you scoundrel, or—

DENNIS
Scoundrel!—Don't be after affronting a housekeeper. Havn't I a sign at my door, three pigs, a wife, and a man sarvant?

FRANK
Well, go on.

DENNIS
Damn the word more will I tell you.

FRANK
Why, you infernal—

DENNIS
Oh, be asy!—see what you get, now, by affronting Mr. Dennis Brulgruddery.

[Searching his Pockets.

I'd have talk'd for an hour, if you had kept a civil tongue in your head!—but now, you may read the letter.

[Giving it.

FRANK
A letter!—stupid booby!—why didn't you give it to me at first?—Yes, it is her hand.

[Opens the Letter.

DENNIS
Stupid!—If you're so fond of letters, you might larn to behave yourself to the postman.

FRANK [Reading and agitated]
—Not going to upbraid you—Couldn't rest at my father's—Trifling assistance—Oh, Heaven! does she then want assistance?—The gentleman who has befriended me—damnation!—the gentleman!—Your unhappy Mary.—Scoundrel that I am!—what is she suffering!—but who, who is this gentleman?—no matter—she is distress'd, heart breaking! and I, who have been the cause;—I, who—here—

[Running to a Writing Table, and opening a Drawer.

Run—fly—despatch!—

DENNIS
He's mad!

FRANK
Say, I will be at your house, myself—remember, positively come, or send, in the course of the day.—In the mean time, take this, and give it to the person who sent you.
Giving a Purse, which he has taken from the Drawer.

DENNIS
A purse!—'faith, and I'll take it.—Do you know how much is in the inside?

FRANK
Psha! no.—No matter.

DENNIS
Troth, now, if I'd trusted a great big purse to a stranger, they'd have call'd it a bit of a bull:—but let you and I count it out between us,—

[Pouring the Money on the Table.

—for, damn him, say I, who would cheat a poor girl in distress, of the value of a rap.—One, two, three, &c.

[Counting.

FRANK
Worthy, honest fellow!

DENNIS
Eleven, twelve, thirteen—

FRANK
I'll be the making of your house, my good fellow.

DENNIS
Damn the Red Cow, sir,—you put me out.—Seventeen, eighteen, nineteen.—Nineteen fat yellow boys, and a seven shilling piece.—Tell them yourself, sir; then chalk them up over the chimney-piece, else you'll forget, you know.

FRANK
O, friend, when honesty, so palpably natural as yours, keeps the account, I care not for my arithmetic.—Fly now,—bid the servants give you any refreshment you chuse; then hasten to execute your commission.

DENNIS
Thank your honour!—good luck to you! I'll taste the beer;—but, by my soul, if the butler comes the Red Cow over me, I'll tell him, I know sweet from sour.
Exit Dennis.

FRANK
Let me read her letter once more.
[Reads]
I am not going to upbraid you; but after I got your letter, I could not rest at my father's, where I once knew happiness and innocence.—I wish'd to have taken a last leave of you, and to beg a trifling assistance;—but the gentleman who has befriended me in my wanderings, would not suffer me to do so; yet I could not help writing, to tell you, I am quitting this neighbourhood for ever!—That you may never know a moment's sorrow, will always be the prayer of
Your unhappy
Mary.
My mind is hell to me! love, sorrow, remorse, and—yes—and jealousy, all distract me:—and no counsellor to advise with; no friend to whom I may—

[Enter **TOM SHUFFLETON**.

FRANK

Tom Shuffleton! you never arrived more apropos in your life.

TOM SHUFFLETON

That's what the women always say to me. I've rumbled on the road, all night, Frank. My bones ache, my head's muzzy—and we'll drink two bottles of claret a-piece, after dinner, to enliven us.

FRANK

You seem in spirits, Tom, I think, now.

TOM SHUFFLETON

Yes;—I have had a windfall—Five hundred pounds.

FRANK

A legacy?

TOM SHUFFLETON

No.—The patient survives who was sick of his money. 'Tis a loan from a friend.

FRANK

'Twould be a pity, then, Tom, if the patient experienced improper treatment.

TOM SHUFFLETON

Why, that's true:—but his case is so rare, that it isn't well understood, I believe. Curse me, my dear Frank, if the disease of lending is epidemic.

FRANK

But the disease of trying to borrow, my dear Tom, I am afraid, is.

TOM SHUFFLETON

Very prevalent, indeed, at the west end of the town.

FRANK

And as dangerous, Tom, as the small-pox. They should inoculate for it.

TOM SHUFFLETON

That wouldn't be a bad scheme; but I took it naturally. Psha! damn it, don't shake your head. Mine's but a mere façon de parler: just as we talk to one another about our coats:—we never say, "Who's your tailor?" We always ask, "Who suffers?" Your father tells me you are going to be married; I give you joy.

FRANK

Joy! I have known nothing but torment, and misery, since this cursed marriage has been in agitation.

TOM SHUFFLETON

Umph! Marriage was a weighty affair, formerly; so was a family coach;—but domestic duties, now, are like town chariots;—they must be made light, to be fashionable.

FRANK

Oh, do not trifle. By acceding to this match, in obedience to my father, I leave to all the pangs of remorse, and disappointed love, a helpless, humble girl, and rend the fibres of a generous, but too credulous heart, by cancelling like a villain, the oaths with which I won it.

TOM SHUFFLETON

I understand:—A snug thing in the country.—Your wife, they tell me, will have four thousand a year.

FRANK

What has that to do with sentiment?

TOM SHUFFLETON

I don't know what you may think; but, if a man said to me, plump, "Sir, I am very fond of four thousand a year;" I should say,—"Sir, I applaud your sentiment very highly."

FRANK

But how does he act, who offers his hand to one woman, at the very moment his heart is engaged to another?

TOM SHUFFLETON

He offers a great sacrifice.

FRANK

And where is the reparation to the unfortunate he has deserted?

TOM SHUFFLETON

An annuity.—A great many unfortunates sport a stylish carriage, up and down St. James's street, upon such a provision.

FRANK

An annuity, flowing from the fortune, I suppose, of the woman I marry! is that delicate?

TOM SHUFFLETON

'Tis convenient. We liquidate debts of play, and usury, from the same resources.

FRANK

And call a crowd of jews and gentlemen gamesters together, to be settled with, during the debtor's honeymoon!

TOM SHUFFLETON

No, damn it, it wouldn't be fair to jumble the jews into the same room with our gaming acquaintance.

FRANK

Why so?

TOM SHUFFLETON

Because, twenty to one, the first half of the creditors would begin dunning the other.

FRANK
Nay, far once in your life be serious. Read this, which has wrung my heart, and repose it, as a secret, in your own.
[Giving the Letter.

TOM SHUFFLETON [Glancing over it]
A pretty, little, crowquill kind of a hand.—"Happiness,—innocence,—trifling assistance—gentleman befriended me—unhappy Mary."—Yes, I see—
[Returning it]
—She wants money, but has got a new friend.—The style's neat, but the subject isn't original.

FRANK
Will you serve me at this crisis?

TOM SHUFFLETON
Certainly.

FRANK
I wish you to see my poor Mary in the course of the day. Will you talk to her?

TOM SHUFFLETON
O yes—I'll talk to her. Where is she to be seen?

FRANK
She writes, you see, that she has abruptly left her father—and I learn, by the messenger, that she is now in a miserable, retired house, on the neighbouring heath.—That mustn't deter you from going.

TOM SHUFFLETON
Me? Oh, dear no—I'm used to it. I don't care how retired the house is.

FRANK
Come down to my father to breakfast. I will tell you afterwards all I wish you to execute.—Oh, Tom! this business has unhinged me for society. Rigid morality, after all, is the best coat of mail for the conscience.

TOM SHUFFLETON
Our ancestors, who wore mail, admired it amazingly; but to mix in the gay world, with their rigid morality, would be as singular as stalking into a drawing-room in their armour:—for dissipation is now the fashionable habit, with which, like a brown coat, a man goes into company, to avoid being stared at.

[Exeunt.

SCENE III

An Apartment in Job Thornberry's House

Enter **JOB THORNBERRY**, in a Night Gown, and **BUR**.

BUR
Don't take on so—don't you, now! pray, listen to reason.

JOB
I won't.

BUR
Pray do!

JOB
I won't. Reason bid me love my child, and help my friend:—what's the consequence? my friend has run one way, and broke up my trade; my daughter has run another, and broke my—No, she shall never have it to say she broke my heart. If I hang myself for grief, she shan't know she made me.

BUR
Well, but, master—

JOB
And reason told me to take you into my shop, when the fat church wardens starved you at the workhouse,—damn their want of feeling for it!—and you were thump'd about, a poor, unoffending, ragged-rump'd boy, as you were—I wonder you hav'n't run away from me too.

BUR
That's the first real unkind word you ever said to me. I've sprinkled your shop two-and-twenty years, and never miss'd a morning.

JOB
The bailiffs are below, clearing the goods: you won't have the trouble any longer.

BUR
Trouble! Lookye, old Job Thornberry—

JOB
Well! What, you are going to be saucy to me, now I'm ruin'd?

BUR
Don't say one cutting thing after another.—You have been as noted, all round our town, for being a kind man, as being a blunt one.

JOB
Blunt or sharp, I've been honest. Let them look at my ledger—they'll find it right. I began upon a little; I made that little great, by industry; I never cringed to a customer, to get him into my books, that I might hamper him with an overcharged bill, for long credit; I earn'd my fair profits; I paid my fair way; I break by the treachery of a friend, and my first dividend will be seventeen shillings in the pound. I wish every tradesman in England may clap his hand on his heart, and say as much, when he asks a creditor to sign his certificate.

BUR

'Twas I kept your ledger, all the time.

JOB

I know you did.

BUR

From the time you took me out of the workhouse.

JOB

Psha! rot the workhouse!

BUR

You never mention'd it to me yourself till to-day.

JOB

I said it in a hurry.

BUR

And I've always remember'd it at leisure. I don't want to brag, but I hope I've been found faithful. It's rather hard to tell poor John Bur, the workhouse boy, after clothing, feeding, and making him your man of trust, for two and twenty years, that you wonder he don't run away from you, now you're in trouble.

JOB [Affected]

John—I beg your pardon.

[Stretching out his Hand.

BUR [Taking his Hand]

Don't say a word more about it.

JOB

I—

BUR

Pray, now, master, don't say any more!—Come, be a man! get on your things; and face the bailiffs that are rummaging the goods.

JOB

I can't, John; I can't. My heart's heavier than all the iron and brass in my shop.

BUR

Nay, consider what confusion!—pluck up a courage; do, now!

JOB

Well, I'll try.

BUR
Aye, that's right: here's your clothes.

[Taking them from the Back of a Chair.

They'll play the devil with all the pots and pans, if you aren't by.—Why, I warrant you'll do! Bless you, what should ail you?

JOB
Ail me? do you go and get a daughter, John Bur; then let her run away from you, and you'll know what ails me.

BUR
Come, here's your coat and waistcoat.

[Going to help him on with his Clothes.

This is the waistcoat young mistress work'd with her own hands, for your birth-day, five years ago. Come, get into it, as quick as you can.

JOB [Throwing it on the Floor violently]
I'd as lieve get into my coffin. She'll have me there soon. Psha! rot it! I'm going to snivel. Bur, go, and get me another.

BUR
Are you sure you won't put it on?

JOB
No, I won't.

[**BUR** pauses.

No, I tell you.—

[Exit **BUR**.

How proud I was of that waistcoat five years ago!—I little thought what would happen now, when I sat in it, at the top of my table, with all my neighbours to celebrate the day;—there was Collop on one side of me, and his wife on the other; and my daughter Mary sat at the farther end;—smiling so sweetly;—like an artful, good for nothing—I shou'dn't like to throw away a waistcoat neither.—I may as well put it on.—Yes—it would be poor spite not to put it on.

[Putting his Arms into it.

—She's breaking my heart; but, I'll wear it, I'll wear it.

[Buttoning it as he speaks, and crying involuntarily.

It's my child's—She's undutiful,—ungrateful,—barbarous,—but she's my child,—and she'll never work me another.

[Enter **BUR**.

BUR
Here's another waistcoat, but it has laid by so long, I think it's damp.

JOB
I was thinking so myself, Bur; and so—

BUR
Eh—what, you've got on the old one? Well, now, I declare, I'm glad of that. Here's your coat.

[Putting it on him.

—'Sbobs! this waistcoat feels a little damp, about the top of the bosom.

JOB [Confused]
Never mind, Bur, never mind.—A little water has dropt on it; but it won't give me cold, I believe.

[A noise without.

BUR
Heigh! they are playing up old Harry below! I'll run, and see what's the matter. Make haste after me, do, now!

[Exit **BUR**.

JOB
I don't care for the bankruptcy now. I can face my creditors, like an honest man; and I can crawl to my grave, afterwards, as poor as a church-mouse. What does it signify? Job Thornberry has no reason now to wish himself worth a groat:—the old ironmonger and brazier has nobody to board his money for now! I was only saving for my daughter; and she has run away from her doating, foolish father,—and struck down my heart—flat—flat.—

[Enter **PEREGRINE**.

Well, who are you?

PEREGRINE
A friend.

JOB
Then, I'm sorry to see you. I have just been ruin'd by a friend; and never wish to have another friend again, as long as I live.—No, nor any ungrateful, undutiful—Poh!—I don't recollect your face.

PEREGRINE

Climate, and years, have been at work on it. While Europeans are scorching under an Indian sun, Time is doubly busy in fanning their features with his wings. But, do you remember no trace of me?

JOB
No, I tell you. If you have any thing to say, say it. I have something to settle below with my daughter—I mean, with the people in the shop;—they are impatient; and the morning has half run away, before she knew I should be up—I mean, before I have had time to get on my coat and waistcoat, she gave me—I mean—I mean, if you have any business, tell it, at once.

PEREGRINE
I will tell it at once. You seem agitated. The harpies, whom I pass'd in your shop, inform'd me of your sudden misfortune, but do not despair yet.

JOB
Aye, I'm going to be a bankrupt—but that don't signify. Go on: it isn't that;—they'll find all fair;—but, go on.

PEREGRINE
I will. 'Tis just thirty years ago, since I left England.

JOB
That's a little after the time I set up in the hardware business.

PEREGRINE
About that time, a lad of fifteen years entered your shop: he had the appearance of a gentleman's son; and told you he had heard, by accident, as he was wandering through the streets of Penzance, some of your neighbours speak of Job Thornberry's goodness to persons in distress.

JOB
I believe he told a lie there.

PEREGRINE
Not in that instance, though he did in another.

JOB
I remember him. He was a fine, bluff, boy!

PEREGRINE
He had lost his parents, he said; and, destitute of friends, money, and food, was making his way to the next port, to offer himself to any vessel that would take him on board, that he might work his way abroad, and seek a livelihood.

JOB
Yes, yes; he did. I remember it.

PEREGRINE
You may remember, too, when the boy had finished his tale of distress, you put ten guineas in his hand. They were the first earnings of your trade, you told him, and could not be laid out to better advantage

than in relieving a helpless orphan;—and, giving him a letter of recommendation to a sea captain at Falmouth, you wished him good spirits, and prosperity. He left you with a promise, that, if fortune ever smil'd upon him, you should, one day, hear news of Peregrine.

JOB
Ah, poor fellow! poor Peregrine! he was a pretty boy. I should like to hear news of him, I own.

PEREGRINE
I am that Peregrine.

JOB
Eh? what—you are—? No: let me look at you again. Are you the pretty boy, that—bless us, how you are alter'd!

PEREGRINE
I have endur'd many hardships since I saw you; many turns of fortune;—but I deceived you (it was the cunning of a truant lad) when I told you I had lost my parents. From a romantic folly, the growth of boyish brains, I had fix'd my fancy on being a sailor, and had run away from my father.

JOB [With great Emotion]
Run away from your father! If I had known that, I'd have horse-whipp'd you, within an inch of your life!

PEREGRINE
Had you known it, you had done right, perhaps.

JOB
Right? Ah! you don't know what it is for a child to run away from a father! Rot me, if I wou'dn't have sent you back to him, tied, neck and heels, in the basket of the stage coach.

PEREGRINE
I have had my compunctions;—have express'd them by letter to my father: but I fear my penitence had no effect.

JOB
Served you right.

PEREGRINE [Sighing]
Having no answers from him, he died, I fear, without forgiving me.

JOB [Starting]
What! died! without forgiving his child!—Come, that's too much. I cou'dn't have done that, neither.— But, go on: I hope you've been prosperous. But you shou'dn't—you shou'dn't have quitted your father.

PEREGRINE
I acknowledge it;—yet, I have seen prosperity; though I traversed many countries, on my outset, in pain and poverty. Chance, at length, raised me a friend in India; by whose interest, and my own industry, I amass'd considerable wealth, in the Factory at Calcutta.

JOB
And have just landed it, I suppose, in England.

PEREGRINE
I landed one hundred pounds, last night, in my purse, as I swam from the Indiaman, which was splitting on a rock, half a league from the neighbouring shore. As for the rest of my property—bills, bonds, cash, jewels—the whole amount of my toil and application, are, by this time, I doubt not, gone to the bottom; and Peregrine is returned, after thirty years, to pay his debt to you, almost as poor as he left you.

JOB
I won't touch a penny of your hundred pounds—not a penny.

PEREGRINE
I do not desire you: I only desire you to take your own.

JOB
My own?

PEREGRINE
Yes; I plunged with this box, last night, into the waves. You see, it has your name on it.

JOB
"Job Thornberry," sure enough. And what's in it?

PEREGRINE
The harvest of a kind man's charity!—the produce of your bounty to one, whom you thought an orphan. I have traded, these twenty years, on ten guineas (which, from the first, I had set apart as yours), till they have become ten thousand: take it; it could not, I find, come more opportunely. Your honest heart gratified itself in administering to my need; and I experience that burst of pleasure, a grateful man enjoys, in relieving my reliever.

[Giving him the Box.

JOB [Squeezes **PEREGRINE'S** Hand, returns the Box, and seems almost unable to utter]
Take it again.

PEREGRINE
Why do you reject it?

JOB
I'll tell you, as soon as I'm able. T'other day, I lent a friend—Pshaw, rot it! I'm an old fool!

[Wiping his Eyes.

—I lent a friend, t'other day, the whole profits of my trade, to save him from sinking. He walk'd off with them, and made me a bankrupt. Don't you think he is a rascal?

PEREGRINE

Decidedly so.

JOB
And what should I be, if I took all you have saved in the world, and left you to shift for yourself?

PEREGRINE
But the case is different. This money is, in fact, your own. I am inur'd to hardships; better able to bear them, and am younger than you. Perhaps, too, I still have prospects of—

JOB
I won't take it. I'm as thankful to you, as if I left you to starve: but I won't take it.

PEREGRINE
Remember, too, you have claims upon you, which I have not. My guide, as I came hither, said, you had married in my absence: 'tis true, he told me you were now a widower; but, it seems, you have a daughter to provide for.

JOB
I have no daughter to provide for now!

PEREGRINE
Then he misinform'd me.

JOB
No, he didn't. I had one last night; but she's gone.

PEREGRINE
Gone!

JOB
Yes; gone to sea, for what I know, as you did. Run away from a good father, as you did.—This is a morning to remember;—my daughter has run out, and the bailiffs have run in;—I shan't soon forget the day of the month.

PEREGRINE
This morning, did you say?

JOB
Aye, before day-break;—a hard-hearted, base—

PEREGRINE
And could she leave you, during the derangement of your affairs?

JOB
She did'nt know what was going to happen, poor soul! I wish she had now. I don't think my Mary would have left her old father in the midst of his misfortunes.

PEREGRINE [Aside]

Mary! it must be she! What is the amount of the demands upon you?

JOB

Six thousand. But I don't mind that: the goods can nearly cover it—let 'em take 'em—damn the gridirons and warming-pans!—I could begin again—but, now, my Mary's gone, I hav'n't the heart; but I shall hit upon something.

PEREGRINE

Let me make a proposal to you, my old friend. Permit me to settle with the officers, and to clear all demands upon you. Make it a debt, if you please. I will have a hold, if it must be so, on your future profits in trade; but do this, and I promise to restore your daughter to you.

JOB

What? bring back my child! Do you know where she is? Is she safe? Is she far off? Is—

PEREGRINE

Will you receive the money?

JOB

Yes, yes; on those terms—on those conditions. But where is Mary?

PEREGRINE

Patience. I must not tell you yet; but, in four-and-twenty hours, I pledge myself to bring her back to you.

JOB

What, here? to her father's house? and safe? Oh, 'sbud! when I see her safe, what a thundering passion I'll be in with her! But you are not deceiving me? You know, the first time you came into my shop, what a bouncer you told me, when you were a boy.

PEREGRINE

Believe me, I would not trifle with you now. Come, come down to your shop, that we may rid it of its present visitants.

JOB

I believe you dropt from the clouds, all on a sudden, to comfort an old, broken-hearted brazier.

PEREGRINE

I rejoice, my honest friend, that I arrived at so critical a juncture; and, if the hand of Providence be in it, 'tis because Heaven ordains, that benevolent actions, like yours, sooner or later, must ever meet their recompense.

[Exeunt.

ACT THE THIRD

SCENE I

Enter **SIR SIMON ROCHDALE** and the **EARL OF FITZ BALAAM**.

SIR SIMON
Believe me, my lord, the man I wish'd most to meet in my library this morning, was the Earl of Fitz Balaam.

LORD FITZ
Thank you, Sir Simon.

SIR SIMON
Your arrival, a day before your promise, gives us such convenient leisure to talk over the arrangements, relative to the marriage of Lady Caroline Braymore, your lordship's daughter, with my son.

LORD FITZ
True, Sir Simon.

SIR SIMON
Then, while Lady Caroline is at her toilet, we'll dash into business at once; for I know your lordship is a man of few words. They tell me, my lord, you have sat in the Upper House, and said nothing but aye and no, there, for these thirty years.

LORD FITZ
I spoke, for more than a minute, in the year of the influenza.

SIR SIMON
Bless me! the epidemic, perhaps, raging among the members, at the moment.

LORD FITZ
Yes;—they cough'd so loud, I left off in the middle.

SIR SIMON
And you never attempted again.

LORD FITZ
I hate to talk much, Sir Simon;—'tis my way; though several don't like it.

SIR SIMON
I do. I consider it as a mark of your lordship's discretion. The less you say, my lord, in my mind, the wiser you are; and I have often thought it a pity, that some noble orators hav'n't follow'd your lordship's example.—But, here are the writings.

[Sitting down with **LORD FITZ BALAAM**, and taking them from the Table.

We must wave ceremony now, my lord; for all this pile of parchment is built on the independent four thousand a year of your daughter, Lady Caroline, on one hand, and your lordship's incumbrances, on the other.

LORD FITZ
I have saddles on my property, Sir Simon.

SIR SIMON
Which saddles, your lordship's property being uncommonly small, look something like sixteen stone upon a poney. The Fitz Balaam estate, for an earl, is deplorably narrow.

LORD FITZ
Yet, it has given security for a large debt.

SIR SIMON
Large, indeed! I can't think how you have contriv'd it. 'Tis the Archbishop of Brobdignag, squeez'd into Tom Thumb's pantaloons.

LORD FITZ
Mine is the oldest estate in England, Sir Simon.

SIR SIMON
If we may judge of age by decay, my lord, it must be very ancient, indeed!—But this goes to something in the shape of supplies.

[Untying the Papers.

"Covenant between Augustus Julius Braymore, Earl of Fitz Balaam, of Cullender Castle, in the county of Cumberland, and Simon Rochdale, Baronet, of Hollyhock House, in the county of Cornwall."—By the by, my lord, considering what an expense attends that castle, which is at your own disposal, and that, if the auctioneer don't soon knock it down, the weather will, I wonder what has prevented your lordship's bringing it to the hammer.

LORD FITZ [Proudly]
The dignity of my ancestors. I have blood in my family, Sir Simon—

SIR SIMON
A deal of excellent blood, my lord; but from the butler down to the house-dog, curse me if ever I saw so little flesh in a family before—But by this covenant—

LORD FITZ
You clear off the largest mortgage.

SIR SIMON
Right;—for which purpose, on the day of the young folks' marriage—

LORD FITZ
You must pay me forty thousand pounds.

SIR SIMON
Right, again. Your lordship says little; but 'tis terribly plump to the point, indeed, my lord. Here is the covenant;—and, now, will your lordship look over the marriage articles?

LORD FITZ
My attorney will be here to-morrow, Sir Simon.
I prefer reading by deputy.

[**BOTH** rise.

SIR SIMON
Many people of rank read in the same way, my lord. And your lordship will receive the forty thousand pounds, I am to pay you, by deputy also, I suppose.

LORD FITZ
I seldom swear, Sir Simon; but, damn me if I will.

SIR SIMON
I believe you are right. Yet there are but two reasons for not trusting an attorney with your money:—one is, when you don't know him very well; and the other is, when you do.—And now, since the marriage is concluded, as I may say, in the families, may I take the liberty to ask, my lord, what sort of a wife my son Frank may expect in Lady Caroline? Frank is rather of a grave, domestic turn: Lady Caroline, it seems, has passed the three last winters in London. Did her ladyship enter into all the spirit of the first circles?

LORD FITZ
She was as gay as a lark, Sir Simon.

SIR SIMON
Was she like the lark in her hours, my lord?

LORD FITZ
A great deal more like the owl, Sir Simon.

SIR SIMON
I thought so. Frank's mornings in London will begin where her ladyship's nights finish. But his case won't be very singular. Many couples make the marriage bed a kind of cold matrimonial well; and the two family buckets dip into it alternately.

[Enter **LADY CAROLINE BRAYMORE**.

LADY CAROLINE
Do I interrupt business?

SIR SIMON
Not in the least. Pray, Lady Caroline, come in. His lordship and I have just concluded.

LORD FITZ
And I must go and walk my three miles, this morning.

SIR SIMON
Must you, my lord?

LORD FITZ
My physician prescribed it, when I told him I was apt to be dull, after dinner.

SIR SIMON
I would attend your lordship;—but since Lady Caroline favours me with—

LADY CAROLINE
No, no—don't mind me. I assure you, I had much rather you would go.

SIR SIMON
Had you?—hum!—but the petticoats have their new school of good breeding, too, they tell me.
[Aside]
Well, we are gone—we have been glancing over the writings, Lady Caroline, that form the basis of my son's happiness:—though his lordship isn't much inclined to read.

LADY CAROLINE
But I am.—I came here to study very deeply, before dinner.

SIR SIMON
What, would your ladyship, then, wish to—

[Showing the Writings.

LADY CAROLINE
To read that? My dear Sir Simon! all that Hebrew, upon parchment as thick as a board!—I came to see if you had any of the last novels in your book room.

SIR SIMON
The last novels!—most of the female new school are ghost bitten, they tell me.
[Aside]
There's Fielding's Works; and you'll find Tom Jones, you know.

LADY CAROLINE
Psha! that's such a hack!

SIR SIMON
A hack, Lady Caroline, that the knowing ones have warranted sound.

LADY CAROLINE
But what do you think of those that have had such a run lately?

SIR SIMON

Why, I think most of them have run too much, and want firing.

[Exeunt **SIR SIMON**, and **LORD FITZ BALAAM**.

LADY CAROLINE
I shall die of ennui, in this moping manor house!—Shall I read to-day?—no, I'll walk.—No, I'll—Yes, I'll read first, and walk afterwards.

[Rings the Bell, and takes a Book.

—Pope.—Come, as there are no novels, this may be tolerable. This is the most triste house I ever saw! [Sits down and reads]
"In these deep solitudes, and awful cells,Where heavenly-pensive—"

[Enter **ROBERT**.

ROBERT
Did you ring, my lady?

LADY CAROLINE
—"Contemplation dwells—" Sir? Oh, yes;—I should like to walk. Is it damp under foot, sir?—"And ever musing—"

ROBERT
There has been a good deal of rain to-day my lady.

LADY CAROLINE
"Melancholy reigns—"

ROBERT
My lady—

LADY CAROLINE
Pray, sir, look out, and bring me word if it is clean or dirty.

ROBERT
Yes, my lady.

[Exit.

LADY CAROLINE
This settling a marriage is a strange business!—"What means this tumult in a vestal's veins?—"

TOM SHUFFLETON [Without]
Bid the groom lead the horse into the avenue, and I'll come to him.

LADY CAROLINE [Resumes her reading]
Company in the house?—some Cornish squire, I suppose.

[Enter **TOM SHUFFLETON**, speaking while entering, **JOHN** following.

LADY CAROLINE [Still reading, and seated with her Back to **SHUFFLETON**]
—"Soon as thy letters, trembling, I unclose—"

JOHN
What horse will you have saddled, sir?

TOM SHUFFLETON
Slyboots.

[Exit **JOHN**.

LADY CAROLINE
—"That well known name awakens all my woes—"

TOM SHUFFLETON
Lady Caroline Braymore!

LADY CAROLINE
Mr. Shuffleton! Lard! what can bring you into Cornwall?

TOM SHUFFLETON
Sympathy:—which has generally brought me near your ladyship, in London at least, for these three winters.

LADY CAROLINE
Psha! but seriously?

TOM SHUFFLETON
I was summoned by friendship. I am consulted on all essential points, in this family;—and Frank Rochdale is going to be married.

LADY CAROLINE
Then, you know to whom?

TOM SHUFFLETON
No;—not thinking that an essential point, I forgot to ask. He kneels at the pedestal of a rich shrine, and I didn't inquire about the statue. But, dear Lady Caroline, what has brought you into Cornwall?

LADY CAROLINE
Me? I'm the statue.

TOM SHUFFLETON
You!

LADY CAROLINE

Yes; I've walk'd off my pedestal, to be worshipp'd at the Land's End.

TOM SHUFFLETON
You to be married to Frank Rochdale! O, Lady Caroline! what then is to become of me?

LADY CAROLINE
Oh, Mr. Shuffleton! not thinking that an essential point, I forgot to ask.

TOM SHUFFLETON
Psha! now you're laughing at me! but upon my soul, I shall turn traitor; take advantage of the confidence reposed in me, by my friend, and endeavour to supplant him.

LADY CAROLINE
What do you think the world would call such duplicity of conduct?

[Enter **ROBERT**.

ROBERT
Very dirty, indeed, my lady.

[Exit.

TOM SHUFFLETON
That infernal footman has been listening!—I'll kick him round his master's park.

LADY CAROLINE
'Tis lucky, then, you are booted; for, you hear, he says it is very dirty there.

TOM SHUFFLETON
Was that the meaning of—Pooh!—but, you see, the—the surprise—the—the agitation has made me ridiculous.

LADY CAROLINE
I see something has made you ridiculous; but you never told me what it was before.

TOM SHUFFLETON
Lady Caroline; this is a crisis, that—my attentions,—that is, the—In short, the world, you know, my dear Lady Caroline, has given me to you.

LADY CAROLINE
Why, what a shabby world it is!

TOM SHUFFLETON
How so?

LADY CAROLINE
To make me a present of something, it sets no value on itself.

TOM SHUFFLETON
I flattered myself I might not be altogether invaluable to your ladyship.

LADY CAROLINE
To me! Now, I can't conceive any use I could make of you. No, positively, you are neither useful nor ornamental.

TOM SHUFFLETON
Yet, you were never at an opera, without me at your elbow;—never in Kensington Gardens, that my horse—the crop, by the bye, given me by Lord Collarbone,—wasn't constantly in leading at the gate:—hav'n't you danc'd with me at every ball?—And hav'nt I, unkind, forgetful, Lady Caroline, even cut the Newmarket meetings, when you were in London?

LADY CAROLINE
Bless me!—these charges are brought in like a bill. "To attending your ladyship at such a time; to dancing down twenty couple with your ladyship, at another,"—and, pray, to what do they all amount?

TOM SHUFFLETON
The fullest declaration.

LADY CAROLINE
Lard, Mr. Shuffleton! why, it has, to be sure, looked a—a—a little foolish—but you—you never spoke any thing to—that is—to justify such a—

TOM SHUFFLETON
That's as much as to say, speak now.
[Aside]
—To be plain, Lady Caroline, my friend does not know your value. He has an excellent heart—but that heart is—
[Coughs]
—damn the word, it's so out of fashion, it chokes me!
[Aside]
—is irrevocably given to another.—But mine—by this sweet hand, I swear—

[Kneeling and kissing her Hand.

[Enter **JOHN**.

Well, sir?—

[Rising hastily.

JOHN
Slyboots, sir, has been down on his knees;—and the groom says he can't go out.

TOM SHUFFLETON
Let him saddle another.

JOHN
What horse, sir, will you—

TOM SHUFFLETON
Psha!—any.—What do you call Mr. Rochdale's favourite, now.

JOHN
Traitor, sir.

TOM SHUFFLETON
When Traitor's in the avenue, I shall be there.

[Exit **JOHN**.

LADY CAROLINE
Answer me one question, candidly, and, perhaps, I may entrust you with a secret.—Is Mr. Rochdale seriously attached?

TOM SHUFFLETON
Very seriously.

LADY CAROLINE
Then I won't marry him.

TOM SHUFFLETON
That's spirited.—Now, your secret.

LADY CAROLINE
Why—perhaps you may have heard, that my father, Lord Fitz Balaam, is, somehow, so—so much in debt, that—but, no matter.

TOM SHUFFLETON
Oh, not at all;—the case is fashionable, with both lords and commoners.

LADY CAROLINE
But an old maiden aunt, whom, rest her soul! I never saw, for family pride's sake, bequeathed me an independence. To obviate his lordship's difficulties, I mean to—to marry into this humdrum Cornish family.

TOM SHUFFLETON
I see—a sacrifice!—filial piety, and all that—to disembarrass his lordship. But hadn't your ladyship better—

LADY CAROLINE
Marry to disembarrass you?

TOM SHUFFLETON
By my honour, I'm disinterested.

LADY CAROLINE
By my honour, I'm monstrously piqued—and so vex'd, that I can't read this morning,—nor talk,—nor—I'll walk.

TOM SHUFFLETON
Shall I attend you?

LADY CAROLINE
No;—don't fidget at my elbow, as you do at the opera. But you shall tell me more of this by and by.

TOM SHUFFLETON [Taking her Hand]
When?—Where?

LADY CAROLINE
Don't torment me.—This evening, or—to-morrow, perhaps;—in the park,—or—psha! we shall meet at dinner.—Do, let me go now, for I shall be very bad company.

TOM SHUFFLETON [Kissing her Hand]
Adieu, Lady Caroline!—

LADY CAROLINE
Adieu!

[Exit.

TOM SHUFFLETON
My friend Frank, here, I think, is very much obliged to me!—I am putting matters pretty well en train to disencumber him of a wife;—and now I'll canter over the heath, and see what I can do for him with the brazier's daughter.

[Exit.

SCENE II

A mean Parlour at the Red Cow

A Table—Pen, Ink, and Paper on it.—Chairs.

MARY and **MRS BRULGRUDDERY** discovered.

MRS BRULGRUDDERY
Aye, he might have been there, and back, over and over again;—but my husband's slow enough in his motions, as I tell him, till I'm tir'd on't.

MARY

I hope he'll be here soon.

MRS BRULGRUDDERY
Ods, my little heart! Miss, why so impatient? Hav'n't you as genteel a parlour as any lady in the land could wish to sit down in?—The bed's turn'd up in a chest of drawers that's stain'd to look like mahogany:—there's two poets, and a poll parrot, the best images the jew had on his head, over the mantlepiece; and was I to leave you all alone by yourself, isn't there an eight day clock in the corner, that when one's waiting, lonesome like, for any body, keeps going tick-tack, and is quite company?

MARY
Indeed, I did not mean to complain.

MRS BRULGRUDDERY
Complain?—No, I think not, indeed!—When, besides having a handsome house over your head, the strange gentleman has left two guineas—though one seems light, and t'other looks a little brummish—to be laid out for you, as I see occasion. I don't say it for the lucre of any thing I'm to make out of the money, but, I'm sure you can't want to eat yet.

MARY
Not if it gives any trouble;—but I was up before sunrise, and have tasted nothing to-day.

MRS BRULGRUDDERY
Eh! why, bless me, young woman! ar'n't you well?

MARY
I feel very faint.

MRS BRULGRUDDERY
Aye, this is a faintish time o'year; but I must give you a little something, I suppose:—I'll open the window, and give you a little air.

DENNIS BRULGRUDDERY [Singing, without]
They handed the whiskey about,
'Till it smoked thro' the jaws of the piper;
The bride got a fine copper snout,
And the clergyman's pimples grew riper.
Whack doodlety bob, Sing pip.

MARY
There's your husband!

MRS BRULGRUDDERY
There's a hog;—for he's as drunk as one, I know, by his beastly bawling.

[Enter **DENNIS BRULGRUDDERY**, singing.

Whack doodlety bob, Sing pip.

MRS BRULGRUDDERY
"Sing pip," indeed! sing sot! and that's to your old tune.

MARY
Hav'n't you got an answer?

MRS BRULGRUDDERY
Hav'n't you got drunk?

DENNIS
Be aisy, and you'll see what I've got in a minute.

[Pulls a Bottle from his Pocket.

MRS BRULGRUDDERY
What's that?

DENNIS
Good Madeira, it was, when the butler at the big house gave it me. It jolts so over the heath, if I hadn't held it to my mouth, I'd have wasted half.

[Puts it on the Table.

—There, Miss, I brought it for you; and I'll get a glass from the cupboard, and a plate for this paper of sweet cakes, that the gentlefolks eat, after dinner in the desert.

MARY
But, tell me if—

DENNIS [Running to the Cupboard]
Eat and drink, my jewel; and my discourse shall serve for the seasoning. Drink now, my pretty one!

[Fills a Glass.

—for you have had nothing, I'll be bound.—Och, by the powers! I know the ways of ould mother Brulgruddery.

MRS BRULGRUDDERY
Old mother Brulgruddery!

DENNIS
Don't mind her;—take your prog;—she'd starve a saint.

MRS BRULGRUDDERY
I starve a saint!

DENNIS

Let him stop at the Red Cow, as plump as a porker, and you'd send him away, in a week, like a weasel.—
Bite maccaroony, my darling!

[Offering the Plate to **MARY**.

MARY
I thank you.

DENNIS
'Faith, no merit of mine; 'twas the butler that stole it:—take some.

[Lets the Plate fall.

Slips by St. Patrick!

MRS BRULGRUDDERY [Screaming]
Our best china plate broke all to shivers!

DENNIS
Delf, you deceiver; delf. The cat's dining dish, rivetted.

MARY
Pray now, let me hear your news.

DENNIS
That I will.—Mrs. Brulgruddery, I take the small liberty of begging you to get out, my lambkin.

MRS BRULGRUDDERY
I shan't budge an inch. She needn't be asham'd of any thing that's to be told, if she's what she should be.

MARY
I know what I should be, if I were in your place.

MRS BRULGRUDDERY
Marry come up! And what should you be then?

MARY
More compassionate to one of my own sex, or to any one in misfortune. Had you come to me, almost broken hearted, and not looking like one quite abandoned to wickedness, I should have thought on your misery, and forgot that it might have been brought on by your faults.

DENNIS
At her, my little crature! By my soul, she'll bother the ould one!—'Faith, the Madeira has done her a deal of service!

MRS BRULGRUDDERY
What's to be said, is said before me; and that's flat.

MARY
Do tell it, then,—
[To **DENNIS**]
—but, for others' sakes, don't mention names. I wish to hide nothing now, on my own account; though the money that was put down for me, before you would afford me shelter, I thought might have given me a little more title to hear a private message.

MRS BRULGRUDDERY
I've a character, for virtue, to lose, young woman.

DENNIS
When that's gone, you'll get another—that's of a damn'd impertinent landlady. Sure, she has a right to her parlour; and hav'n't I brought her cash enough to swallow up the Red Cow's rent for these two years?

MRS BRULGRUDDERY
Have you!—Well, though the young lady misunderstands me, it's always my endeavour to be respectful to gentlefolks.

DENNIS
Och, botheration to the respect that's bought, by knocking one shilling against another, at an inn! Let the heart keep open house, I say; and if charity is not seated inside of it, like a beautiful barmaid, it's all a humbug to stick up the sign of the christian.

MRS BRULGRUDDERY
I'm sure Miss shall have any thing she likes, poor dear thing! There's one chicken—

DENNIS
A chicken!—Fie on your double barbarity! Would you murder the tough dunghill cock, to choke a customer?—A certain person, that shall be nameless, will come to you in the course of this day, either by himself, or by friend, or by handwriting.

MARY
And not one word—not one, by letter, now?

DENNIS
Be asey—won't he be here soon? In the mean time, here's nineteen guineas, and a seven shilling piece, as a bit of a postscript.

MRS BRULGRUDDERY
Nineteen guineas and—

DENNIS
Hold your gab, woman.—Count them, darling!—

[Putting them on the Table—**MARY** counts the Money.

MRS BRULGRUDDERY [Drawing **DENNIS**]

What have you done with the rest?

DENNIS
The rest!

MRS BRULGRUDDERY
Why, have you given her all?

DENNIS
I'll tell you what, Mrs. Brulgruddery; it's my notion, in summing up your last accounts, that, when you begin to dot, ould Nick will carry one; and that's yourself, my lambkin.

TOM SHUFFLETON [Without]
Holo? Red Cow!

DENNIS
You are call'd, Mrs. Brulgruddery.

MRS BRULGRUDDERY
I, you Irish bear!—Go, and—

[Looking towards the window.

—Jimminy! a traveller on horseback! and the handsomest gentleman I ever saw in my life.

[Runs out.

MARY
Oh, then it must be he!

DENNIS
No, 'faith, it isn't the young squire.

MARY [Mournfully]
No!

DENNIS
There—he's got off the outside of his horse: it's that flashy spark I saw crossing the court yard, at the big house.—Here he is.

[Enter **TOM SHUFFLETON**.

TOM SHUFFLETON [Looking at **MARY**]
Devilish good-looking girl, upon my soul!

[Sees **DENNIS**.

Who's that fellow?

DENNIS
Welcome to Muckslush Heath, sir.

TOM SHUFFLETON
Pray, sir, have you any business, here?

DENNIS
Very little this last week, your honour.

TOM SHUFFLETON
O, the landlord. Leave the room.

DENNIS [Aside]
Manners! but he's my customer. If he don't behave himself to the young cratur, I'll bounce in, and thump him blue.

[Exit.

TOM SHUFFLETON [Looking at **MARY**]
Shy, but stylish—much elegance, and no brass: the most extraordinary article that ever belonged to a brazier.—
[Addressing her]
Don't be alarmed, my dear. Perhaps you didn't expect a stranger?

MARY
No, sir.

TOM SHUFFLETON
But you expected somebody, I believe, didn't you?

MARY
Yes, sir.

TOM SHUFFLETON
I come from him: here are my credentials. Read that, my dear little girl, and you'll see how far I am authorized.

[Gives her a Letter.

MARY
'Tis his hand.

[Kissing the Superscription.

TOM SHUFFLETON [As she is opening the Letter]
Fine blue eyes, faith, and very like my Fanny's. Yes, I see how it will end;—she'll be the fifteenth Mrs. Shuffleton.

MARY [Reading]
When the conflicts of my mind have subsided, and opportunity will permit, I will write to you fully. My friend is instructed from me to make every arrangement for your welfare. With heartfelt grief I add, family circumstances have torn me from you for ever!—

[Drops the Letter, and is falling, **SHUFFLETON** supports her.

TOM SHUFFLETON
Ha! damn it, this looks like earnest! They do it very differently in London.

MARY [Recovering]
I beg pardon, sir—I expected this; but I—I—

[Bursts into Tears.

TOM SHUFFLETON [Aside]
O, come, we are getting into the old train; after the shower, it will clear.—My dear girl, don't flurry yourself;—these are things of course, you know. To be sure, you must feel a little resentment at first, but—

MARY
Resentment! When I am never, never to see him again! Morning and night, my voice will be raised to Heaven, in anguish, for his prosperity!—And tell him,—pray, sir, tell him, I think the many, many bitter tears I shall shed, will atone for my faults; then you know, as it isn't himself, but his station, that sunders us, if news should reach him that I have died, it can't bring any trouble to his conscience.

TOM SHUFFLETON
Mr. Rochdale, my love, you'll find will be very handsome.

MARY
I always found him so, sir.

TOM SHUFFLETON
He has sent you a hundred pound bank note—

[Giving it to her.

—till matters can be arranged, just to set you a-going.

MARY
I was going, sir, out of this country, for ever. Sure he couldn't think it necessary to send me this, for fear I should trouble him!

TOM SHUFFLETON
Pshaw! my love, you mistake: the intention is to give you a settlement.

MARY

I intended to get one for myself, sir.

TOM SHUFFLETON
Did you?

MARY
Yes, sir, in London. I shall take a place in the coach to-morrow morning; and I hope the people of the inn where it puts up, at the end of the journey, will have the charity to recommend me to an honest service.

TOM SHUFFLETON
Service? Nonsense! You—you must think differently. I'll put you into a situation in town.

MARY
Will you be so humane, sir?

TOM SHUFFLETON
Should you like Marybone parish, my love?

MARY
All parishes are the same to me, now I must quit my own, sir.

TOM SHUFFLETON
I'll write a line for you, to a lady in that quarter, and—Oh, here's pen and ink.

[Writes, and talks as he is writing.

I shall be in London myself, in about ten days, and then I'll visit you, to see how you go on.

MARY
O sir! you are, indeed a friend!

TOM SHUFFLETON
I mean to be your friend, my love. There,

[Giving her the Letter.

Mrs. Brown, Howland-Street; an old acquaintance of mine; a very goodnatured, discreet, elderly lady, I assure you.

MARY
You are very good, sir, but I shall be ashamed to look such a discreet person in the face, if she hears my story.

TOM SHUFFLETON
No, you needn't;—she has a large stock of charity for the indiscretions of others, believe me.

MARY
I don't know how to thank you, sir. The unfortunate must look up to such a lady, sure, as a mother.

TOM SHUFFLETON
She has acquired that appellation.—You'll be very comfortable;—and, when I arrive in town, I'll—

[Enter **PEREGRINE**.

Who have we here?
[Aside]
—Oh!—ha!—ha!—This must be the gentleman she mentioned to Frank in her letter.—rather an ancient ami.

PEREGRINE
So! I suspected this might be the case.
[Aside]
You are Mr. Rochdale, I presume sir?

TOM SHUFFLETON
Yes, sir, you do presume;—but I am not Mr. Rochdale.

PEREGRINE
I beg your pardon, sir, for mistaking you for so bad a person.

TOM SHUFFLETON
Mr. Rochdale, sir, is my intimate friend. If you mean to recommend yourself in this quarter,—
[Pointing to **MARY**]
—good breeding will suggest to you, that it mustn't be done by abusing him, before me.

PEREGRINE
I have not acquired that sort of good breeding, sir, which isn't founded on good sense;—and when I call the betrayer of female innocence a bad character, the term, I think, is too true to be abusive.

TOM SHUFFLETON
'Tis a pity, then, you hav'n't been taught a little better, what is due to polished society.

PEREGRINE
I am always willing to improve.

TOM SHUFFLETON
I hope, sir, you won't urge me to become your instructor.

PEREGRINE
You are unequal to the task: if you quarrel with me in the cause of a seducer, you are unfit to teach me the duties of a citizen.

TOM SHUFFLETON
You may make, sir, a very good citizen; but, curse me, if you'll do for the west end of the town.

PEREGRINE

I make no distinctions in the ends of towns, sir:—the ends of integrity are always uniform: and 'tis only where those ends are most promoted, that the inhabitants of a town, let them live east or west, most preponderate in rational estimation.

TOM SHUFFLETON
Pray, sir, are you a methodist preacher, in want of a congregation?

PEREGRINE
Perhaps I'm a quack doctor, in want of a Jack Pudding.—Will you engage with me?

TOM SHUFFLETON
Damn me if this is to be borne.—Sir, the correction I must give you, will—

PEREGRINE [With Coolness]
Desist, young man, in time, or you may repent your petulance.

MARY [Coming between them]
Oh, gentlemen! pray, pray don't—I am so frightened! Indeed, sir, you mistake.
[To **PEREGRINE**]
This gentleman has been so good to me!

[Pointing to **SHUFFLETON**.

PEREGRINE
Prove it, child, and I shall honour him.

MARY
Indeed, indeed he has.—Pray, pray don't quarrel! when two such generous people meet, it would be a sad pity. See, sir,—
[To **PEREGRINE**]
—he has recommended me to a place in London;—here's the letter to the good lady, an elderly lady, in Marybone parish! and so kind, sir, every body, that knows her, calls her mother.

PEREGRINE [Looking at the superscription]
Infamous! sit down, and compose yourself, my love;—the gentleman and I shall soon come to an understanding. One word, sir:
[**MARY** sits at the back of the Scene, the **MEN** advance]
I have lived long in India;—but the flies, who gad thither, buzz in our ears, till we learn what they have blown upon in England. I have heard of the wretch, in whose house you meant to place that unfortunate.

TOM SHUFFLETON
Well! and you meant to place her in snugger lodgings, I suppose?

PEREGRINE
I mean to place her where—

TOM SHUFFLETON

No, my dear fellow, you don't;—unless you answer it to me.

PEREGRINE
I understand you.—In an hour, then, I shall be at the Manor-house, whence I suppose, you come. Here we are both unarmed; and there is one waiting at the door, who, perhaps, might interrupt us.

TOM SHUFFLETON
Who is he?

PEREGRINE
Her father;—her agonized father;—to whose entreaties I have yielded; and brought him here, prematurely.—He is a tradesman;—beneath your notice:—a vulgar brazier;—but he has some sort of feeling for his child! whom, now your friend has lured her to the precipice of despair, you would hurry down the gulf of infamy.—For your own convenience, sir, I would advise you to avoid him.

TOM SHUFFLETON
Your advice, now, begins to be a little sensible; and if you turn out a gentleman, though I suspect you to be one of the brazier's company, I shall talk to you at Sir Simon's.

[Exit.

MARY
Is the gentleman gone, sir?

PEREGRINE
Let him go, child; and be thankful that you have escaped from a villain.

MARY
A villain, sir!

PEREGRINE
The basest; for nothing can be baser than manly strength, in the specious form of protection, injuring an unhappy woman. When we should be props to the lily in the storm, 'tis damnable to spring up like vigorous weeds, and twine about the drooping flower, till we destroy it.

MARY
Then, where are friends to be found, sir? He seemed honest; so do you; but, perhaps, you may be as bad.

PEREGRINE
Do not trust me. I have brought you a friend, child, in whom, Nature tells us, we ever should confide.

MARY
What, here, sir?

PEREGRINE
Yes;—when he hurts you, he must wound himself;—and so suspicious is the human heart become, from the treachery of society, that it wants that security. I will send him to you.

[Exit.

MARY
Who can he mean? I know nobody but Mr. Rochdale, that, I think, would come to me. For my poor dear father, when he knows all my crime, will abandon me, as I deserve.

[Enter **JOB THORNBERRY**, at the Door **PEREGRINE** has gone out at.

JOB
Mary!

[**MARY** shrieks and falls, her **FATHER** runs to her.

My dear Mary!—Speak to me!

MARY [Recovering]
Don't look kindly on me, my dear father! Leave me; I left you:—but I was almost mad.

JOB
I'll never leave you, till I drop down dead by your side. How could you run away from me, Mary?

[She shrieks.

Come, come, kiss me, and we'll talk of that another time.

MARY
You hav'n't heard half the story, or I'm sure you'd never forgive me.

JOB
Never mind the story now, Mary;—'tis a true story that you're my child, and that's enough for the present. I hear you have met with a rascal. I hav'n't been told who, yet. Some folks don't always forgive; braziers do. Kiss me again, and we'll talk on't by and by. But, why would you run away, Mary?

MARY
I could'nt stay and be deceitful; and it has often cut me to the heart, to see you show me that affection, which I knew I didn't deserve.

JOB
Ah! you jade! I ought to be angry; but I can't. Look here—don't you remember this waistcoat? you worked it for me, you know.

MARY [Kissing him]
I know I did.

JOB

I had a hard struggle to put it on, this morning; but I squeezed myself into it, a few hours after you ran away.—If I could do that, you might have told me the worst, without much fear of my anger. How have they behaved to you, Mary?

MARY
The landlord is very humane, but the landlady—

JOB
Cruel to you? I'll blow her up like gunpowder in a copper. We must stay here to-night;—for there's Peregrine, that king of good fellows, we must stay here till he comes back, from a little way off, he says.

MARY
He that brought you here?

JOB
Ay, he. I don't know what he intends—but I trust all to him;—and when he returns, we'll have such a merry-making! Hollo! house! Oh, damn it, I'll be good to the landlord; but I'll play hell with his wife! Come with me, and let us call about us a bit. Hollo!—house! Come, Mary! odsbobs, I'm so happy to have you again! House!—Come, Mary.

[Exeunt.

ACT THE FOURTH

SCENE I

The Outside of the Red Cow

DENNIS BRULGRUDDERY before the Door.

DENNIS
I've stretched my neck half a yard longer, looking out after that rapscallion,
DAN
Och! and is it yourself I see, at last? There he comes, in a snail's trot, with a basket behind him, like a stage coach.

[Enter **DAN**, with a Basket at his Back.

Dan, you devil! aren't you a beast of a waiter?

DAN
What for?

DENNIS
To stay out so, the first day of company.

DAN

Come, that be a good un! I ha' waited for the company a week, and I defy you to say I ever left the house till they comed.

DENNIS

Well, and that's true. Pacify me with a good reason, and you'll find me a dutiful master. Arrah, Dan, what's that hump grown out at your back, on the road?

DAN

Plenty o' meat and drink. I ha'n't had such a hump o' late, at my stomach.

[Puts the Basket on the Ground.

DENNIS

And who harnessed you, Dan, with all that kitchen stuff?

DAN

He as ware rack'd, and took I wi' un to Penzance, for a companion. He order'd I, as I said things were a little famish'd like, here, to buy this for the young woman, and the old man he ha' brought back wi' un.

DENNIS

Then you have been gabbling your ill looking stories about my larder, you stone eater!

DAN

Larder! I told un you had three live pigs as ware dying.

DENNIS

Oh fie! Think you, won't any master discharge a man sarvant that shames him? Thank your luck, I can't blush. But is the old fellow, our customer has brought, his intimate friend, he never saw but once, thirty years ago?

DAN

Ees; that be old Job Thornberry, the brazier; and, as sure as you stand there, when we got to his shop, they were going to make him a banker.

DENNIS

A banker! I never saw one made. How do they do it?

DAN

Why, the bum baileys do come into his house, and claw away all his goods and furniture.

DENNIS

By the powers, but that's one way of setting a man going in business!

DAN

When we got into the shop, there they were, as grum as thunder.—You ha' seen a bum bailey?

DENNIS

I'm not curious that way. I might have seen one, once or twice; but I was walking mighty fast, and had no time to look behind me.

DAN

My companion—our customer—he went up stairs, and I bided below;—and then they began a knocking about the goods and chapels.—That ware no business o' mine.

DENNIS

Sure it was not.

DAN

Na, for sartin; so I ax'd 'em what they were a doing;—and they told I, wi' a broad grin, taking an invention of the misfortunate man's defects.

DENNIS

Choke their grinning! The law of the land's a good doctor; but, bad luck to those that gorge upon such a fine physician's poor patients! Sure, we know, now and then, it's mighty wholesome to bleed; but nobody falls in love with the leech.

DAN

They comed down stairs—our customer and the brazier; and the head baily he began a bullocking at the old man, in my mind, just as one christian shou'dn't do to another. I had nothing to do wi' that.

DENNIS

Damn the bit.

DAN

No, nothing at all; and so my blood began to rise. He made the poor old man almost fit to cry.

DENNIS

That wasn't your concern, you know.

DAN

Bless you, mun! 'twould ha' look'd busy like, in me, to say a word; so I took up a warming pan, and I bang'd bum bailey, wi' the broad end on't, 'till he fell o' the floor as fat as twopence.

DENNIS

Oh, hubaboo! lodge in my heart, and I'll never ax you for rent—you're a friend in need. Remember, I've a warmingpan—you know where it hangs, and that's enough.

DAN

They had like to ha' warm'd I, finely, I do know. I ware nigh being haul'd to prison; 'cause, as well as I could make out their cant, it do seem I had rescued myself, and broke a statue.

DENNIS

Och, the Philistines!

DAN

But our traveller—I do think he be the devil—he settled all in a jiffy; for he paid the old man's debts, and the bailey's broken head ware chuck'd into the bargain.

DENNIS
And what did he pay?

DAN
Guess now.

DENNIS
A hundred pounds?

DAN
Six thousand, by gum!

DENNIS
What! on the nail?

DAN
Na; on the counter.

DENNIS
Whew!—six thousand pou—! Oh, by the powers, this man must be the philosopher's stone! Dan—

DAN
Hush! here he be.

[Enter **PEREGRINE**, from the House.

PEREGRINE [To **DAN**]
So, friend, you have brought provision, I perceive.

DAN
Ees, sir;—three boil'd fowls, three roast, two chicken pies, and a capon.

PEREGRINE
You have considered abundance, more than variety. And the wine?

DAN
A dozen o' capital red port, sir: I ax'd for the newest they had i' the cellar.

DENNIS [To himself]
Six thousand pounds upon a counter!

PEREGRINE [To **DAN**]
Carry the hamper in doors; then return to me instantly. You must accompany me in another excursion.

DAN

What, now?

PEREGRINE
Yes; to Sir Simon Rochdale's. You are not tired, my honest fellow?

DAN
Na, not a walking wi' you;—but, dang me, when you die, if all the shoemakers shouldn't go into mourning.

[**DAN** takes the Hamper into the House.

DENNIS [Ruminating]
Six thousand pounds! by St. Patrick, it's a sum!

PEREGRINE
How many miles from here to the Manor house?

DENNIS
Six thousand!

PEREGRINE
Six thousand!—yards you mean, I suppose, friend.

DENNIS
Sir!—Eh? Yes, sir, I—I mean yards—all upon a counter!

PEREGRINE
Six thousand yards upon a counter! Mine host, here, seems a little bewildered;—but he has been anxious, I find, for poor Mary, and 'tis national in him to blend eccentricity with kindness. John Bull exhibits a plain, undecorated dish of solid benevolence; but Pat has a gay garnish of whim around his good nature; and if, now and then, 'tis sprinkled in a little confusion, they must have vitiated stomachs, who are not pleased with the embellishment.

[Enter **DAN**, booted.

DAN
Now, sir, you and I'll stump it.

PEREGRINE
Is the way we are to go now, so much worse, that you have cased yourself in those boots?

DAN
Quite clean—that's why I put 'em on: I should ha' dirted 'em in t' other job.

PEREGRINE
Set forward, then.

DAN

Na, sir, axing your pardon; I be but the guide, and 'tisn't for I to go first.

PEREGRINE
Ha! ha! Then we must march abreast, boy, like lusty soldiers, and I shall be side by side with honesty: 'tis the best way of travelling through life's journey, and why not over a heath? Come, my lad.

DAN
Cheek by jowl, by gum!

[Exeunt **PEREGRINE** and **DAN**.

DENNIS
That walking philosopher—perhaps he'll give me a big bag of money. Then, to be sure, I won't lay out some of it to make me easy for life: for I'll settle a separate maintenance upon ould mother Brulgruddery.

[**JOB THORNBERRY** peeps out of the Door of the Public House.

JOB
Landlord!

DENNIS
Coming, your honour.

JOB [Coming forward]
Hush! don't bawl;—Mary has fallen asleep. You have behaved like an emperor to her, she says. Give me your hand, landlord.

DENNIS
Behaved!—Arrah, now, get away with your blarney.

[Refusing his Hand.

JOB
Well, let it alone. I'm an old fool, perhaps; but, as you comforted my poor girl in her trouble, I thought a squeeze from her father's hand—as much as to say, "Thank you, for my child."—might not have come amiss to you.

DENNIS
And is it yourself who are that creature's father?

JOB
Her mother said so, and I always believed her. You have heard some'at of what has happen'd, I suppose. It's all over our town, I take it, by this time. Scandal is an ugly, trumpeting devil. Let 'em talk;—a man loses little by parting with a herd of neighbours, who are busiest in publishing his family misfortunes; for they are just the sort of cattle who would never stir over the threshold to prevent 'em.

DENNIS

Troth, and that's true;—and some will only sarve you, because you're convenient to 'em, for the time present; just as my customers come to the Red Cow.

JOB
I'll come to the Red Cow, hail, rain, or shine, to help the house, as long as you are Landlord. Though I must say that your wife—

DENNIS [Putting his Hand before **JOB'S** Mouth]
Decency! Remember your own honour, and my feelings. I mustn't hear any thing bad, you know, of Mrs. Brulgruddery; and you'll say nothing good of her, without telling damn'd lies; so be asy.

JOB
Well, I've done;—but we mustn't be speaking ill of all the world, neither: there are always some sound hearts to be found among the hollow ones. Now he that is just gone over the heath—

DENNIS
What, the walking philosopher?

JOB
I don't know any thing of his philosophy; but, if I live these thousand years, I shall never forget his goodness. Then, there's another;—I was thinking, just now, if I had tried him, I might have found a friend in my need, this morning.

DENNIS
Who is he?

JOB
A monstrous good young man; and as modest and affable, as if he had been bred up a 'prentice, instead of a gentleman.

DENNIS
And what's his name?

JOB
Oh, every body knows him, in this neighbourhood; he lives hard by—Mr. Francis Rochdale, the young 'squire, at the Manor-house.

DENNIS
Mr. Francis Rochdale!

JOB
Yes!—he's as condescending! and took quite a friendship for me, and mine. He told me, t'other day, he'd recommend me in trade to all the great families twenty miles round;—and said he'd do, I don't know what all, for my Mary.

DENNIS
He did!—Well, 'faith, you may'nt know what; but, by my soul, he has kept his word!

JOB
Kept his word!—What do you mean?

DENNIS
Harkye—If Scandal is blowing about your little fireside accident, 'twas Mr. Francis Rochdale recommended him to your shop, to buy his brass trumpet.

JOB [Bawling]
Eh! What? no!—yes—I see it at once!—young Rochdale's a rascal!—Mary!

DENNIS
Hush—you'll wake her, you know.

JOB
I intend it. I'll—a glossy, oily, smooth rascal!—warming me in his favour, like an unwholesome February sun! shining upon my poor cottage, and drawing forth my child,—my tender blossom,—to suffer blight, and mildew!—Mary! I'll go directly to the Manor-house—his father's in the commission.—I may'nt find justice, but I shall find a justice of peace.

DENNIS
Fie, now! and can't you listen to reason?

JOB
Reason!—tell me a reason why a father shouldn't be almost mad, when his patron has ruin'd his child.—Damn his protection!—tell me a reason why a man of birth's seducing my daughter doesn't almost double the rascality? yes, double it: for my fine gentleman, at the very time he is laying his plans to make her infamous, would think himself disgraced in making her the honest reparation she might find from one of her equals.

DENNIS
Arrah, be asy, now, Mr. Thornberry.

JOB
And, this spark, forsooth, is now canvassing the county!—but, if I don't give him his own at the hustings!—How dare a man set himself up for a guardian of his neighbour's rights, who has robbed his neighbour of his dearest comforts? How dare a seducer come into freeholders' houses, and have the impudence to say, send me up to London as your representative? Mary!

DENNIS
That's all very true.—But if the voters are under petticoat government, he has a mighty good chance of his election.

[Enter **MARY**.

MARY
Did you call, my dear father?

JOB [Passionately]

Yes, I did call.

DENNIS
Don't you frighten that poor young crature!

MARY
Oh, dear! what has happened?—You are angry; very angry. I hope it isn't with me!—if it is, I have no reason to complain.

JOB [Softened, and folding her in his Arms]
My poor, dear child! I forgive you twenty times more, now, than I did before.

MARY
Do you, my dear father?

JOB
Yes; for there's twenty times more excuse for you, when rank and education have helped a scoundrel to dazzle you. Come!

[Taking her Hand.

MARY
Come! where?

JOB [Impatiently]
To the Manor-house with me, directly.

MARY
To the Manor-house! Oh, my dear father, think of what you are doing! think of me!

JOB
Of you!—I think of nothing else. I'll see you righted. Don't be terrified, child—damn it, you know I doat on you: but we are all equals in the eye of the law; and rot me, if I won't make a baronet's son shake in his shoes, for betraying a brazier's daughter. Come, love, come!
Exeunt Job and Mary.

DENNIS
There'll be a big boderation at the Manor-house! My customers are all gone, that I was to entertain:—nobody's left but my lambkin, who don't entertain me: Sir Simon's butler gives good Madeira:—so, I'm off, after the rest; and the Red Cow and mother Brulgruddery may take care of one another.

[Exit.

SCENE II

Enter **FRANK ROCHDALE**.

FRANK
Shuffleton's intelligence astonishes me!—So soon to throw herself into the arms of another!—and what could effect, even if time for perseverance had favoured him, such a person's success with her!

[Enter **SIR SIMON ROCHDALE**.

SIR SIMON
Why, Frank! I thought you were walking with Lady Caroline.

FRANK
No, sir.

SIR SIMON
Ha! I wish you would learn some of the gallantries of the present day from your friend, Tom Shuffleton:—but from being careless of coming up to the fashion, damn it, you go beyond it? for you neglect a woman three days before marriage, as much as half the Tom Shuffletons three months after it.

FRANK
As by entering into this marriage, sir, I shall perform the duties of a son, I hope you will do me the justice to suppose I shall not be basely negligent as a husband,

SIR SIMON
Frank, you're a fool; and—

[Enter a **SERVANT**.

Well, sir?

SERVANT
A person, Sir Simon, says he wishes to see you on very urgent business.

SIR SIMON
And I have very urgent business, just now, with my steward. Who is the person? How did he come?
Serv. On foot, Sir Simon.

SIR SIMON
Oh, let him wait.

[Exit **SERVANT**.

At all events, I can't see this person for these two hours.—I wish you would see him for me.

FRANK [Aside, and going]
Certainly, sir,—any thing is refuge to me, now, from the subject of matrimony.

SIR SIMON

But a word before you go. Damn it, my dear lad, why can't you perceive I am labouring this marriage for your good? We shall ennoble the Rochdales:—for, though my father,—your grandfather,—did some service in elections (that made him a baronet), amassed property, and bought lands, and so on, yet, your great grandfather—Come here—
[Half whispering]
—your great grandfather was a miller.

FRANK [Smiling]
I shall not respect his memory less, sir, for knowing his occupation.

SIR SIMON
But the world will, you blockhead: and, for your sake, for the sake of our posterity, I would cross the cart breed, as much as possible, by blood.

FRANK
Is that of consequence, sir?

SIR SIMON
Isn't it the common policy? and the necessities of your boasters of pedigree produce a thousand intermarriages with people of no pedigree at all;—till, at last, we so jumble a genealogy, that, if the devil himself would pluck knowledge from the family tree, he could hardly find out the original fruit.

[Exeunt **SEVERALLY**.

[Enter **TOM SHUFFLETON**, from the Park, following **LADY CAROLINE BRAYMORE**.

TOM SHUFFLETON
"The time is come for Iphigene to find,
"The miracle she wrought upon my mind;"

LADY CAROLINE
Don't talk to me.

TOM SHUFFLETON
"For, now, by love, by force she shall be mine,
"Or death, if force should fail, shall finish my design."

LADY CAROLINE
I wish you would finish your nonsense.

TOM SHUFFLETON
Nonsense:—'tis poetry; somebody told me 'twas written by Dryden.

LADY CAROLINE
Perhaps so;—but all poetry is nonsense.

TOM SHUFFLETON
Hear me, then, in prose.

LADY CAROLINE
Psha!—that's worse.

TOM SHUFFLETON
Then I must express my meaning in pantomime. Shall I ogle you?

LADY CAROLINE
You are a teasing wretch;—I have subjected myself, I find, to very ill treatment, in this petty family;—and begin to perceive I am a very weak woman.

TOM SHUFFLETON [Aside]
Pretty well for that matter.

LADY CAROLINE
To find myself absolutely avoided by the gentleman I meant to honour with my hand,—so pointedly neglected!—

TOM SHUFFLETON
I must confess it looks a little like a complete cut.

LADY CAROLINE
And what you told me of the low attachment that—

TOM SHUFFLETON
Nay, my dear Lady Caroline, don't say that I told you more than—

LADY CAROLINE
I won't have it denied:—and I'm sure 'tis all true. See here—here's an odious parchment Lord Fitz Balaam put into my hand in the park.—A marriage license, I think he calls it—but if I don't scatter it in a thousand pieces—

TOM SHUFFLETON [Preventing her]
Softly, my dear Lady Caroline; that's a license of marriage, you know. The names are inserted of course.—Some of them may be rubbed a little in the carriage; but they may be filled up at pleasure, you know.—Frank's my friend,—and if he has been negligent, I say nothing; but the parson of the parish is as blind as a beetle.

LADY CAROLINE
Now, don't you think, Mr. Shuffleton, I am a very ill used person?

TOM SHUFFLETON
I feel inwardly for you, Lady Caroline; but my friend makes the subject delicate. Let us change it. Did you observe the steeple upon the hill, at the end of the park pales?

LADY CAROLINE
Psha?—No.

TOM SHUFFLETON
It belongs to one of the prettiest little village churches you ever saw in your life. Let me show you the inside of the church, Lady Caroline.

LADY CAROLINE
I am almost afraid: for, if I should make a rash vow there, what is to become of my Lord Fitz Balaam?

TOM SHUFFLETON
Oh, that's true; I had forgot his lordship:—but as the exigencies of the times demand it, let us hurry the question through the Commons, and when it has passed, with such strong independent interest on our sides, it will hardly be thrown out by the Peerage.

[Exeunt.

SCENE III

Another Apartment in Sir Simon Rochdale's House

[Enter **PEREGRINE**.

PEREGRINE
Sir Simon does not hurry himself; but 'tis a custom with the great, to make the little, and the unknown, dance attendance. When I left Cornwall, as a boy, this house, I remember, was tenanted by strangers, and the Rochdales inhabited another on the estate, seven miles off.—I have lived to see some changes in the family, and may live, perhaps, to see more.

[Enter **FRANK ROCHDALE**.

FRANK
You expected, I believe, Sir Simon Rochdale, sir;—but he will be occupied with particular business, for some time. Can I receive your commands, sir?

PEREGRINE
Are you Sir Simon Rochdale's son, sir?

FRANK
I am.

PEREGRINE
It was my wish, sir, to have seen your father. I come unintroduced, and scurvily enough accoutred; but, as I have urgent matters to communicate, and have suffered shipwreck, upon your coast, this morning, business will excuse my obtrusion, and the sea must apologize for my wardrobe.

FRANK
Shipwreck! That calamity is a sufficient introduction to every roof, I trust, in a civilized country. What can we do immediately to serve you?

PEREGRINE
Nothing, sir—I am here to perform service, not to require it. I come from a wretched hut on the heath, within the ken of this affluent mansion, where I have witnessed calamity in the extreme.

FRANK
I do not understand you.

PEREGRINE
Mary!—

FRANK
Ha.!—Now you have made me understand you. I perceive, now, on what object you have presented yourself here, to harangue. 'Tis a subject on which my own remorse would have taught me to bend to a just man's castigation; but the reproof retorts on the reprover, when he is known to be a hypocrite. My friend, sir, has taught me to know you.

PEREGRINE
He, whom I encountered at the house on the heath?

FRANK
The same.

PEREGRINE
And what may he have taught you?

FRANK
To discover, that your aim is to torture me, for relinquishing a beloved object, whom you are, at this moment, attaching to yourself;—to know, that a diabolical disposition, for which I cannot account, prompts you to come here, without the probability of benefiting any party, to injure me, and throw a whole family into confusion, on the eve of a marriage. But, in tearing myself from the poor, wronged, Mary, I almost tear my very heart by its fibres from the seat;—but 'tis a sacrifice to a father's repose; and—

PEREGRINE
Hold, sir! When you betrayed the poor, wronged, Mary, how came you to forget, that every father's repose may be broken for ever by his child's conduct?

FRANK
By my honour! by my soul! it was my intention to have placed her far, far above the reach of want; but you, my hollow monitor, are frustrating that intention. You, who come here to preach virtue, are tempting her to be a confirmed votary of vice, whom I in penitence would rescue, as the victim of unguarded sensibility.

PEREGRINE
Are you, then, jealous of me?

FRANK

Jealous!

PEREGRINE
Aye: if so, I can give you ease. Return with me, to the injured innocent on the heath: marry her, and I will give her away.

FRANK
Marry her! I am bound in honour to another.

PEREGRINE
Modern honour is a coercive argument; but when you have seduced virtue, whose injuries you will not solidly repair, you must be slightly bound in old-fashion'd honesty.

FRANK
I—I know not what to say to you. Your manner almost awes me; and there is a mystery in—

PEREGRINE
I am mysterious, sir. I may have other business, perhaps, with your father; and, I will tell you, the very fate of your family may hang on my conference with him. Come, come, Mr. Rochdale, bring me to Sir Simon.

FRANK
My father cannot be seen yet. Will you, for a short time, remain in my apartment?

PEREGRINE
Willingly;—and depend on this, sir—I have seen enough of the world's weakness, to forgive the casual faults of youthful indiscretion;—but I have a detestation for systematic vice; and though, as a general censor, my lash may be feeble, circumstances have put a scourge in my hand, which may fall heavily on this family, should any of its branches force me to wield it.—I attend you.

[Exeunt.

ACT THE FIFTH

SCENE I

A Hall in the Manor-house

VOICES wrangling without.

JOB
I will see Sir Simon.

SIR SIMON
You can't see Sir Simon, &c. &c. &c.
Enter Job Thornberry, Mary, and Simon.

JOB
Don't tell me;—I come upon justice business.

SIR SIMON
Sir Simon be a gentleman justice.

JOB
If the justice allows all his servants to be as saucy as you, I can't say much for the gentleman.

SIR SIMON
But these ben't his hours.

JOB
Hours for justice! I thought one of the blessings of an Englishman, was to find justice at any time.

MARY
Pray don't be so—

JOB
Hold your tongue, child. What are his hours?

SIR SIMON
Why, from twelve to two.

JOB
Two hours out of four and twenty! I hope all that belong to law, are a little quicker than his worship; if not, when a case wants immediate remedy, it's just eleven to one against us. Don't you know me?

SIR SIMON
Na.

JOB
I'm sure I have seen you in Penzance.

SIR SIMON
My wife has got a chandler's shop there.

JOB
Haven't you heard we've a fire engine in the church?

SIR SIMON
What o' that?

JOB
Suppose your wife's shop was in flames, and all her bacon and farthing candles frying?

SIR SIMON

And what then?

JOB
Why then, while the house was burning, you'd run to the church for the engine. Shou'dn't you think it plaguy hard if the sexton said, "Call for it to-morrow, between twelve and two?"

SIR SIMON
That be neither here nor there.

JOB [Menacing]
Isn't it! Then, do you see this stick?

SIR SIMON
Pshaw! you be a foolish old fellow.

JOB
Why, that's true. Every now and then a jack-in-office, like you, provokes a man to forget his years. The cudgel is a stout one, and som'at like your master's justice;—'tis a good weapon in weak hands; and that's the way many a rogue escapes a dressing.—What! you are laughing at it?

SIR SIMON
Ees.

JOB
Ees! you Cornish baboon, in a laced livery!—Here's something to make you grin more—here's half a crown.

[Holding it up between his Finger and Thumb.

SIR SIMON
Hee! hee!

JOB
Hee, hee!—Damn your Land'send chops! 'tis to get me to your master:—but, before you have it, though he keeps a gentleman-justice-shop, I shall make free to ring it on his counter.

[Throws it on the Floor.

There! pick it up.

[**SIR SIMON** picks up the money.

I am afraid you are not the first underling that has stoop'd to pocket a bribe, before he'd do his duty.—Now, tell the gentleman-justice, I want to see him.

SIR SIMON
I'll try what I can do for you.

[Exit.

JOB
What makes you tremble so, Mary?

MARY
I can't help it:—I wish I could persuade you to go back again.

JOB
I'll stay till the roof falls, but I'll see some of 'em.

MARY
Indeed, you don't know how you terrify me. But, if you go to Sir Simon, you'll leave me here in the hall;—you won't make me go with you, father?

JOB
Not take you with me.—I'll go with my wrongs in my hand, and make him blush for his son.

MARY
I hope you'll think better of it.

JOB
Why?

MARY
Because, when you came to talk, I should sink with shame, if he said any thing to you that might—that—

JOB
Might what?

MARY [Sighing, and hanging down her Head]
Make you blush for your daughter.

JOB
I won't have you waiting, like a petitioner, in this hall, when you come to be righted. No, no!

MARY
You wouldn't have refused me any thing once;—but I know I have lost your esteem, now.

JOB
Lost!—forgive is forgive, all the world over. You know, Mary, I have forgiven you: and, making it up by halves, is making myself a brass teakettle—warm one minute, cold the next; smooth without, and hollow within.

MARY
Then, pray, don't deny me!—I'm sure you wouldn't, if you knew half I am suffering.

JOB

Do as you like, Mary; only never tell me again you have lost my esteem. It looks like suspicion o' both sides.—Never say that, and I can deny you nothing in reason,—or, perhaps, a little beyond it.—

[Enter **SIR SIMON**.

Well, will the justice do a man the favour to do his duty? Will he see me?

SIR SIMON
Come into the room next his libery. A stranger, who's with young master, ha' been waiting for un, longer nor you; but I'll get you in first.

JOB
I don't know, that that's quite fair to the other.

SIR SIMON
Ees, it be; for t'other didn't give I half a crown.

JOB
Then, stay till I come back, Mary.—I see, my man, when you take a bribe, you are scrupulous enough to do your work for it; for which, I hope, somebody may duck you with one hand, and rub you dry with the other. Kindness and honesty, for kindness and honesty's sake, is the true coin; but many a one, like you, is content to be a passable Birmingham halfpenny.

[Exeunt **JOB THORNBERRY** and **SIR SIMON**.

MARY
I wished to come to this house in the morning, and now I would give the world to be out of it. Hark! here's somebody! Oh, mercy on me, 'tis he himself! What will become of me!

[Retires towards the Back of the Scene.

[Enter **FRANK ROCHDALE**.

FRANK
My father, then, shall see this visitor, whatever be the event. I will prepare him for the interview, and—
[Sees **MARY**]
Good Heaven! why—why are you here?

MARY [Advancing to him eagerly]
I don't come willingly to trouble you; I don't, indeed!

FRANK
What motive, Mary, has brought you to this house? and who is the stranger under whose protection you have placed yourself, at the house on the heath? Surely you cannot love him!

MARY
I hope I do.

FRANK
You hope you do!

MARY
Yes; for I think he saved my life this morning, when I was struggling with the robber, who threatened to kill me.

FRANK
And had you taken no guide with you, Mary?—no protector?

MARY
I was thinking too much of one, who promised to be my protector always, to think of any other.

FRANK
Mary—I—I—'twas I, then, it seems who brought your life into such hazard.

MARY
I hope I haven't said any thing to make you unhappy.

FRANK
Nothing, my dearest Mary, nothing. I know it is not in your nature even to whisper a reproof. Yet, I sent a friend, with full power from me, to give you the amplest protection.

MARY
I know you did:—and he gave me a letter, that I might be protected, when I got to London.

FRANK
Why, then, commit yourself to the care of a stranger?

MARY
Because the stranger read the direction of the letter—here it is,—

[Taking it from her Pocket.

—and said your friend was treacherous.

FRANK [Looking at the Letter]
Villain!

MARY
Did he intend to lead me into a snare then?

FRANK
Let me keep this letter.—I may have been deceived in the person I sent to you, but—damn his rascality! [Aside]
But, could you think me base enough to leave you, unsheltered? I had torn you from your home,—with anguish I confess it—but I would have provided you another home, which want should not have assailed. Would this stranger bring you better comfort?

MARY

Oh, yes; he has; he has brought me my father.

FRANK

Your father!—from whom I made you fly!

MARY

Yes; he has brought a father to his child,—that she might kiss off the tears her disobedience had forced down his aged cheeks, and restored me to the only home, which could give me any comfort, now.—And my father is here.

FRANK

Here!

MARY

Indeed, I cou'dn't help his coming; and he made me come with him.

FRANK

I—I am almost glad, Mary, that it has happened.

MARY

Are you?

FRANK

Yes—when a weight of concealment is on the mind, remorse is relieved by the very discovery which it has dreaded. But you must not be waiting here,

MARY

There is one in the house, to whose care I will entrust you.

MARY

I hope it isn't the person you sent to me to-day.

FRANK

He! I would sooner cradle infancy with serpents.—Yet this is my friend! I will, now, confide in a stranger:—the stranger, Mary, who saved your life.

MARY

Is he here!

FRANK

He is:—Oh, Mary, how painful, if, performing the duty of a son, I must abandon, at last, the expiation of a penitent! but so dependent on each other are the delicate combinations of probity, that one broken link perplexes the whole chain, and an abstracted virtue becomes a relative iniquity.

[Exeunt.

The Library

SIR SIMON ROCHDALE and his **STEWARD**, who appears to be quitting the Room. **JOB THORNBERRY** standing at a little Distance from them.

SIR SIMON
Remember the money must be ready to-morrow, Mr. Pennyman.

STEWARD
It shall, Sir Simon.

[Going.

SIR SIMON [To **JOB**]
So, friend, your business, you say, is—and, Mr. Pennyman,—
[**STEWARD** turns back]
—give Robin Ruddy notice to quit his cottage, directly.

STEWARD
I am afraid, Sir Simon, if he's turned out, it will be his ruin.

SIR SIMON
He should have recollected that, before he ruin'd his neighbour's daughter.

JOB [Starting]
Eh!

SIR SIMON
What's the matter with the man? His offence is attended with great aggravation.—Why doesn't he marry her?

JOB [Emphatically]
Aye!

SIR SIMON
Pray, friend, be quiet.

STEWARD
He says it would make her more unfortunate still; he's too necessitous to provide even for the living consequence of his indiscretion.

SIR SIMON
That doubles his crime to the girl.—He must quit. I'm a magistrate, you know, Mr. Pennyman, and 'tis my duty to discourage all such immorality.

STEWARD
Your orders must be obeyed, Sir Simon.

[Exit **STEWARD**.

SIR SIMON
Now, yours is justice-business, you say. You come at an irregular time, and I have somebody else waiting for me; so be quick. What brings you here?

JOB
My daughter's seduction, Sir Simon;—and it has done my heart good to hear your worship say, 'tis your duty to discourage all such immorality.

SIR SIMON
To be sure it is;—but men, like you, shou'dn't be too apt to lay hold of every sentiment justice drops, lest you misapply it. 'Tis like an officious footman snatching up his mistress's periwig, and clapping it on again, hind part before. What are you?

JOB
A tradesman, Sir Simon.
I have been a freeholder, in this district, for many a year.

SIR SIMON
A freeholder!—Zounds! one of Frank's voters, perhaps, and of consequence at his election.
[Aside]
Won't you, my good friend, take a chair?

JOB
Thank you, Sir Simon, I know my proper place. I didn't come here to sit down with Sir Simon Rochdale, because I am a freeholder; I come to demand my right, because you are a justice.

SIR SIMON
A man of respectability, a tradesman, and a freeholder, in such a serious case as yours, had better have recourse to a court of law.

JOB
I am not rich, now, Sir Simon, whatever I may have been.

SIR SIMON
A magistrate, honest, friend, can't give you damages:—you must fee counsel.

JOB
I can't afford an expensive lawsuit, Sir Simon:—and, begging your pardon, I think the law never intended that an injured man, in middling circumstances, should either go without redress, or starve himself to obtain it.

SIR SIMON

Whatever advice I can give you, you shall have it for nothing; but I can't jump over justice's hedges and ditches. Courts of law are broad high roads, made for national convenience; if your way lie through them, 'tis but fair you should pay the turnpikes. Who is the offender?

JOB
He lives on your estate, Sir Simon.

SIR SIMON
Oho! a tenant!—Then I may carry you through your journey by a short cut. Let him marry your daughter, my honest friend.

JOB
He won't.

SIR SIMON
Why not?

JOB
He's going to marry another.

SIR SIMON
Then he turns out. The rascal sha'n't disgrace my estate four and twenty hours longer.—Injure a reputable tradesman, my neighbour!—a freeholder!—and refuse to—did you say he was poor?

JOB
No, Sir Simon; and, by and by, if you don't stand in his way, he may be very rich.

SIR SIMON
Rich! eh!—Why, zounds! is he a gentleman?

JOB
I have answer'd that question already, Sir Simon.

SIR SIMON
Not that I remember.

JOB
I thought I had been telling you his behaviour.

SIR SIMON
Umph!

JOB
I reckon many of my neighbours honest men, though I can't call them gentlemen;—but I reckon no man a gentleman, that I can't call honest.

SIR SIMON

Harkye, neighbour;—if he's a gentleman (and I have several giddy young tenants, with more money than thought), let him give you a good round sum, and there's an end.

JOB
A good round sum!—Damn me, I shall choke!
[Aside]
A ruffian, with a crape, puts a pistol to my breast, and robs me of forty shillings;—a scoundrel, with a smiling face, creeps to my fireside, and robs my daughter of her innocence. The judge can't allow restitution to spare the highwayman;—then, pray, Sir Simon,—I wish to speak humbly—pray don't insult the father, by calling money a reparation from the seducer.

SIR SIMON
This fellow must be dealt with quietly I see—Justice, my honest friend, is—justice.—As a magistrate, I make no distinction of persons.—Seduction is a heinous offence: and, whatever is in my power, I—

JOB
The offender is in your power, Sir Simon.

SIR SIMON
Well, well; don't be hasty, and I'll take cognizance of him.—We must do things in form:—but you mustn't be passionate.

[Goes to the Table, and takes up a Pen.

Come, give me his christian and surname, and I'll see what's to be done for you.—Now, what name must I write?

JOB
Francis Rochdale.

SIR SIMON [Drops the Pen, looks at Job, and starts up]
Damn me! if it isn't the brazier!

JOB
Justice is justice, Sir Simon. I am a respectable tradesman, your neighbour, and a freeholder.—Seduction is a heinous offence; a magistrate knows no distinction of persons; and a rascal musn't disgrace your estate four and twenty hours longer.

SIR SIMON [Sheepishly]
I believe your name is Thornberry?

JOB
It is, Sir Simon. I never blush'd at my name, till your son made me blush for yours.

SIR SIMON
Mr. Thornberry—I—I heard something of my son's—a—little indiscretion, some mornings ago.

JOB

Did you, Sir Simon? you never sent to me about it; so, I suppose, the news reach'd you at one of the hours you don't set apart for justice.

SIR SIMON
This is a—a very awkward business, Mr. Thornberry. Something like a hump back;—we can never set it quite straight, so we must bolster it.

JOB
How do you mean, Sir Simon?

SIR SIMON
Why—'tis a—a disagreeable affair, and—we—must hush it up.

JOB
Hush it up! a justice compound with a father, to wink at his child's injuries! if you and I hush it up so, Sir Simon, how shall we hush it up here?

[Striking his Breast.

In one word, will your son marry my daughter?

SIR SIMON
What! my son marry the daughter of a brazier!

JOB
He has ruined the daughter of a brazier.—If the best lord in the land degrades himself by a crime, you can't call his atonement for it a condescension.

SIR SIMON
Honest friend—I don't know in what quantities you may sell brass at your shop; but when you come abroad, and ask a baronet to marry his son to your daughter, damn me, if you ar'n't a wholesale dealer!

JOB
And I can't tell, Sir Simon, how you may please to retail justice; but when a customer comes to deal largely with you, damn me if you don't shut up the shop windows!

SIR SIMON
You are growing saucy. Leave the room, or I shall commit you.

JOB
Commit me! you will please to observe, Sir Simon, I remember'd my duty, till you forgot yours. You asked me, at first, to sit down in your presence. I knew better than to do so, before a baronet and a justice of peace. But I lose my respect for my superior in rank, when he's so much below my equals in fair dealing:—and, since the magistrate has left the chair—

[Slams the Chair into the middle of the Room.

—I'll sit down on it.

[Sits down.

There!—'Tis fit it should be fill'd by somebody—and, dam'me if I leave the house till you redress my daughter, or I shame you all over the county!

SIR SIMON
Why, you impudent mechanic! I shou'dn't wonder if the scoundrel call'd for my clerk, and sign'd my mittimus.

[Rings the Bell.

Fellow, get out of that chair.

JOB
I sha'n't stir. If you want to sit down, take another. This is the chair of justice: it's the most uneasy for you of any in the room.

[Enter **SERVANT**.

SIR SIMON
Tell Mr. Rochdale to come to me directly.

SERVANT
Yes,

SIR SIMON [Sees **JOB**]
Hee! hee!

SIR SIMON
Don't stand grinning, you booby! but go.

SERVANT
Yes,

SIR SIMON
Hee! he!

[Exit.

JOB [Reaching a Book from the Table]
"Burn's Justice!"

SIR SIMON
And how dare you take it up?

JOB
Because you have laid it down. Read it a little better, and, then, I may respect you more.—There it is.

[Throws it on the Floor.

[Enter **FRANK ROCHDALE**.

SIR SIMON
So, sir! prettily I am insulted on your account!

FRANK
Good Heaven, sir! what is the matter?

SIR SIMON
The matter!
[Points to **JOB**]
Lug that old bundle of brass out of my chair, directly.

[**FRANK** casts his Eyes on **THORNBERRY**, then on the Ground, and stands abashed.

JOB
He dare as soon jump into one of your tin-mines. Brass!—there is no baser metal than hypocrisy: he came with that false coin to my shop, and it pass'd; but see how conscience nails him to the spot, now!

FRANK [To **SIR SIMON**]
Sir, I came to explain all.

SIR SIMON
Sir, you must be aware that all is explained already. You provoke a brazier almost to knock me down; and bring me news of it, when he is fix'd as tight in my study, as a copper in my kitchen.

FRANK [Advancing to **JOB**]
Mr. Thornberry, I—

JOB
Keep your distance! I'm an old fellow; but if my daughter's seducer comes near me, I'll beat him as flat as a stewpan.

FRANK [Still advancing]
Suffer me to speak, and—

JOB [Rising from the Chair, and holding up his Cane]
Come an inch nearer, and I'll be as good as my word.

[Enter **PEREGRINE**.

PEREGRINE
Hold!

JOB

Eh! you here? then I have some chance, perhaps, of getting righted, at last.

PEREGRINE
Do not permit passion to weaken that chance.

JOB
Oh, plague! you don't know;—I wasn't violent till—

PEREGRINE
Nay, nay; cease to grasp that cane.—While we are so conspicuously bless'd with laws to chastise a culprit, the mace of justice is the only proper weapon for the injured.—Let me talk with you.

[Takes **THORNBERRY** aside.

SIR SIMON [To **FRANK ROCHDALE**]
Well, sir; who may this last person be, whom you have thought proper should visit me?

FRANK
A stranger in this country, sir, and—

SIR SIMON
And a friend, I perceive, of that old ruffian.

FRANK
I have reason to think, sir, he is a friend to Mr. Thornberry.

SIR SIMON
Sir, I am very much obliged to you.—You send a brazier to challenge me, and now, I suppose, you have brought a travelling tinker for his second. Where does he come from?

FRANK
India, sir. He leap'd from the vessel that was foundering on the rocks, this morning, and swam to shore.

SIR SIMON
Did he? I wish he had taken the jump with the brazier tied to his neck.

[**PEREGRINE** and **JOB** come forward.

PEREGRINE [Apart to **JOB**]
I can discuss it better in your absence. Be near with Mary: should the issue be favourable, I will call you.

JOB [Apart to **PEREGRINE**]
Well, well! I will. You have a better head at it than I.—Justice! Oh, if I was Lord Chancellor, I'd knock all the family down with the mace, in a minute.

[Exit.

PEREGRINE

Suffer me to say a few words, Sir Simon Rochdale, in behalf of that unhappy man.

[Pointing to where **JOB** was gone out.

SIR SIMON
And pray, sir, what privilege have you to interfere in my domestic concerns?

PEREGRINE
None, as it appears abstractedly. Old Thornberry has just deputed me to accommodate his domestic concerns with you: I would, willingly, not touch upon yours.

SIR SIMON
Poh! poh! You can't touch upon one, Without being impertinent about the other.

PEREGRINE
Have the candour to suppose, Sir Simon, that I mean no disrespect to your house. Although I may stickle, lustily, with you, in the cause of an aggrieved man, believe me, early habits have taught me to be anxious for the prosperity of the Rochdales.

SIR SIMON
Early habits!

PEREGRINE
I happened to be born on your estate, Sir Simon; and have obligations to some part of your family.

SIR SIMON
Then, upon my soul, you have chosen a pretty way to repay them!

PEREGRINE
I know no better way of repaying them, than by consulting your family honour. In my boyhood, it seem'd as if nature had dropp'd me a kind of infant subject on your father's Cornish territory; and the whole pedigree of your house is familiar to me.

SIR SIMON
Is it? Confound him, he has heard of the miller!
[Aside]
Sir, you may talk this tolerably well; but 'tis my hope—my opinion, I mean, you can't tell who was my grandfather.

PEREGRINE
Whisper the secret to yourself, Sir Simon; and let reason also whisper to you, that, when honest industry raises a family to opulence and honours, its very original lowness sheds lustre on its elevation;—but all its glory fades, when it has given a wound, and denies a balsam, to a man, as humble, and as honest, as your own ancestor.

SIR SIMON [To **FRANK**, who has retired, during the above Conversation, to the Back of the Room]
But I haven't given the wound.—And why, good sir, won't you be pleased to speak your sentiments!

FRANK

The first are, obedience to my father, sir; and, if I must proceed, I own that nothing, in my mind, but the amplest atonement, can extinguish true remorse for a cruelty.

SIR SIMON

Ha! in other words, you can't clap an extinguisher upon your feelings, without a father-in-law who can sell you one. But Lady Caroline Braymore is your wife, or I am no longer your father.

[Enter **TOM SHUFFLETON** and **LADY CAROLINE BRAYMORE**.

TOM SHUFFLETON

How d'ye do, good folks? How d'ye do?

SIR SIMON

Ha! Lady Caroline!—Tom, I have had a little business.—The last dinner-bell has rung, Lady Caroline; but I'll attend you directly.

TOM SHUFFLETON

Baronet, I'm afraid we sha'n't be able to dine with you to-day.

SIR SIMON

Not dine with me!

LADY CAROLINE

No;—we are just married!

SIR SIMON

Hell and the devil! married!

TOM SHUFFLETON

Yes; we are married, and can't come.

PEREGRINE [Aside]

Then 'tis time to speak to old Thornberry.

[Exit.

SIR SIMON

Lady Caroline!

LADY CAROLINE

I lost my appetite in your family this morning, Sir Simon; and have no relish for any thing you can have the goodness to offer me.

TOM SHUFFLETON

Don't press us, baronet;—that's quite out, in the New School.

SIR SIMON

Oh, damn the New School!—who will explain all this mystery?

FRANK
Mr. Shuffleton shall explain it, sir; and other mysteries too.

TOM SHUFFLETON
My dear Frank, I have something to say to you. But here comes my papa; I've been talking to him, Sir Simon, and he'll talk to you. He does very well to explain, for the benefit of a country gentleman.

[Enter **LORD FITZ BALAAM**.

SIR SIMON
My Lord, it is painful to be referred to you, when so much is to be said. What is it all?

LORD FITZ
You are disappointed, Sir Simon, and I am ruin'd.

SIR SIMON
But, my lord—

[They go up the Stage.

[**LADY CAROLINE** throws herself carelessly into a Chair. **TOM SHUFFLETON** advances to **FRANK**.

TOM SHUFFLETON
My dear Frank, I—I have had a devilish deal of trouble in getting this business off your hands. But you see, I have done my best for you.

FRANK
For yourself, you mean.

TOM SHUFFLETON
Come, damn it, my good fellow, don't be ungrateful to a friend.

FRANK
Take back this letter of recommendation, you wrote for Mary, as a friend. When you assume that name with me, Mr. Shuffleton, for myself I laugh; for you I blush; but for sacred friendship's profanation I grieve.

[Turns from him.

TOM SHUFFLETON
That all happens from living so much out of town.

[Enter **PEREGRINE, JOB THORNBERRY**, and **MARY**.

PEREGRINE

Now, Sir Simon, as accident seems to have thwarted a design, which probity could never applaud, you may, perhaps, be inclined to do justice here.

JOB
Justice is all I come for—damn their favours! Cheer up, Mary!

SIR SIMON [To **PEREGRINE**]
I was in hopes I had got rid of you. You are an orator from the sea-shore; but you must put more pebbles in your mouth before you harangue me into a tea-kettle connexion.

TOM SHUFFLETON
That's my friend at the Red Cow. He is the new-old cher ami to honest tea-kettle's daughter.

FRANK
Your insinuation is false, sir.

TOM SHUFFLETON
False!

[Stepping forward.

LADY CAROLINE
Hush! don't quarrel;—we are only married to-day.

TOM SHUFFLETON
That's true; I won't do any thing to make you unhappy for these three weeks.

PEREGRINE
Sir Simon Rochdale, if my oratory fail, and which, indeed, is weak, may interest prevail with you?

SIR SIMON
No; rather than consent, I'd give up every acre of my estate.

PEREGRINE
Your conduct proves you unworthy of your estate; and, unluckily for you, you have roused the indignation of an elder brother, who now stands before you, and claims it.

SIR SIMON
Eh!—Zounds!—Peregrine!

PEREGRINE
I can make my title too good, in an instant, for you to dispute it. My agent in London has long had documents on the secret he has kept; and several old inhabitants here, I know, are prepared to identify me.

SIR SIMON
I had a run-away brother—a boy that every body thought dead. How came he not to claim till now?

PEREGRINE
Because, knowing he had given deep cause of offence, he never would have asserted his abandon'd right, had he not found a brother neglecting, what no Englishman should neglect—justice and humanity to his inferiors.

[Enter **DENNIS BRULGRUDDERY**.

DENNIS
Stand asy, all of you; for I've big news for my half-drown'd customer. Och! bless your mug! and is it there you are?

SIR SIMON
What's the matter now?

DENNIS [To **PEREGRINE**]
Hould your tongue, you little man!—There's a great post just come to your Manor-house, and the Indiaman's work'd into port.

JOB
What, the vessel with all your property?

DENNIS
By all that's amazing, they say you have a hundred thousand pounds in that ship.

PEREGRINE
My losses might have been somewhat more without this recovery. I have entered into a sort of partnership with you, my friend, this morning. How can we dissolve it?

JOB
You are an honest man; so am I; so settle that account as you like.

PEREGRINE
Come forth, then, injured simplicity;—of your own cause you shall be now the arbitress.

MARY
Do not make me speak, sir, I am so humbled—so abash'd—

JOB
Nonsense! we are sticking up for right.

PEREGRINE
Will you then speak, Mr. Rochdale?

FRANK
My father is bereft of a fortune, sir; but I must hesitate till his fiat is obtained, as much as if he possess'd it.

SIR SIMON

Nay, nay; follow your own inclinations now

FRANK
May I, sir? Oh, then, let the libertine now make reparation, and claim a wife.

[Running to **MARY**, and embracing her.

DENNIS
His wife! Och! what a big dinner we'll have at the Red Cow!

PEREGRINE [To **SIR SIMON**]
What am I to say, sir?

SIR SIMON
Oh! you are to say what you please.

PEREGRINE
Then, bless you both! And, tho' I have passed so much of my life abroad, brother, English equity is dear to my heart. Respect the rights of honest John Bull, and our family concerns may be easily arranged.

JOB
That's upright. I forgive you, young man, for what has passed; but no one deserves forgiveness, who refuses to make amends, when he has disturb'd the happiness of an Englishman's fireside.

George Colman the Younger – A Concise Bibliography

The Female Dramatist (1782)
Two to One (1784)
Turk and No Turk (1785)
Inkle and Yarico (1787)
Ways and Means (1788)
The Battle of Hexham (1793)
The Iron Chest (1796)
The Heir at Law (1797)
The Poor Gentleman (1802)
John Bull, or an Englishman's Fireside (1803)

Colman was also the author of a great deal of so-called humorous poetry (usually coarse, though popular) – My Night Gown and Slippers (1797), reprinted under the name of Broad Grins, in 1802; and Poetical Vagaries (1812). Some of his writings were published under the assumed name of Arthur Griffinhood of Turnham Green.

www.ingramcontent.com/pod-product-compliance
Lightning Source LLC
Chambersburg PA
CBHW021935040426
42448CB00008B/1085